SUCCEEDING IN DIVERSITY
culture, language and learning
in primary classrooms

SUCCEEDING IN DIVERSITY
culture, language and learning in primary classrooms

Jean Conteh

Trentham Books

Stoke on Trent, UK and Sterling, USA

Trentham Books Limited

Westview House	22883 Quicksilver Drive
734 London Road	Sterling
Oakhill	VA 20166-2012
Stoke on Trent	USA
Staffordshire	
England ST4 5NP	

First published 2003. Reprinted 2008.

British Library Cataloguing-in-Publication Data
A catalogue record for this book is available from the British Library

1 85856 294 5

Designed and typeset by Trentham Print Design Ltd., Chester and printed in Great Britain by Cpod, Trowbridge, Wiltshire.

CONTENTS

ACKNOWLEDGEMENTS

This book is the result of years of learning and teaching in many different contexts, but mainly in Bradford and in the Department of Teacher Education at Bradford College. I am especially grateful to colleagues in the Language and Literature strand through the years for their friendship and generous support and for their abiding belief in the importance of succeeding in diversity.

I am grateful to the children, their parents and their teachers who gave me their time and their trust and some of whose words appear in the book; particularly Rehamat Bibi, Bilal Butt, Sabiha Butt, Kramat Hussain, Rashida Hussain, Sannah Hussain, Shabnam Hussain, Sehrish Mirza, Shahida Mirza, Jenny Prudom and Julie Waterhouse. Thanks also go to the students and teachers who gave me permission to quote from their work. I have lost touch with 'Rukhsana', part of whose story appears on page 22. I hope she feels I have interpreted her words correctly. Thanks also to Sara Ali for help with translation from Urdu.

I owe much to the persistence and editorial expertise of Gillian Klein and the scholarship and enthusiasm of Eve Gregory. I am also indebted to the friendly critical readers who read some or all of the book in draft form and offered much helpful feedback and advice – not all of which I followed: Aamir Darr, Ishrat Iqbal, Norah McWilliam, Barry Miller, Peter Pool and Saiqa Riasat. The errors and omissions in the final text are wholly my own.

Last, but certainly not least, thanks as always to my family – Peter, Moi and Feimatta – for their love, encouragement and patience.

I would like to dedicate this book – with hopes for the future – to all the students and teachers in Sierra Leone from whom I learned so much in the optimistic days of the 1970s and 1980s.

If yu no sabi usai yu de go, yu fɔ sabi usai yu kɔmɔt. (If you don't know where you're going, you need to know where you're coming from – Krio proverb from Sierra Leone)

INTRODUCTION

This book is for primary teachers, teacher trainers and students on primary education courses. It is about language and learning, about the ways in which the two interact and the ways in which these interactions are always mediated through, in and by culture. I became interested in these ideas through my experiences of living and working in Sierra Leone, West Africa in the 1970s and early 1980s, and since then in Bradford, West Yorkshire. Much of the content of the book was gathered as part of research I carried out over a number of years while working as a primary teacher trainer. The book describes the learning experiences of a small group of successful bilingual learners as they progress through Key Stage Two in mainstream classrooms. The children are all of Pakistani Muslim heritage. They are the third and fourth generation descendants of the migrants from South Asia who began to arrive in Bradford and similar cities in the north of England in the 1940s, searching for work and a new life.

All the children and their parents and teachers whose words are quoted extensively in this book have been given pseudonyms in order to respect and maintain their privacy. But I decided not to attempt to anonymise the city in which they all live and work, and where I have lived for the past fourteen years. I decided that it was important to present the history and something of the current situation in Bradford as openly as possible for two main reasons. First of all, Bradford is a fascinating place with a rich and distinctive history which strongly influences life and education in the city today in many ways. This, in itself, is a story that deserves to be told. Second, the citizens of Bradford have dealt with issues of diversity and difference over many years. Its communities have had a long history of accepting 'immigrants', and they have done this in active and interesting – and sometimes in contrary – ways. Teachers and students elsewhere in the UK, and in other parts of the world, will surely find aspects of their own situations which resonate with our experiences in Bradford.

The book tells the children's personal stories, often using their own words and those of their parents and teachers. It provides many examples of their interactions with family, friends and teachers in home and at school. With supporting evidence of the experiences, views and attitudes of their parents and teachers, the book shows the ways that successful bilingual and bicultural learners move confidently between social worlds, cultures and languages in their daily lives. I argue that the skills and strategies displayed by the children in all of these interactions need to be recognised and valued in classroom pedagogy and in assessing their achievements in school. If such recognition is not given, there is a danger that we will continue systematically to condemn children from minority ethnic backgrounds to failure in mainstream classrooms. I raise implications from the children's stories for education policy, teacher education and classroom practice, pointing out the parallels with children whose own 'differences' may vary from those I discuss in the book. Finally, I make some practical suggestions for primary teachers and teacher trainers on ways to promote 'success in diversity' in their classrooms.

The book has seven chapters. The first chapter, through practical examples and stories from my own experiences of learning and teaching, sets out the theoretical bases for the rest of the book. It discusses the links between language, culture and learning which underpin the content of the whole book and presents arguments for a view of learning as a socio-cultural process, as very much a dialogue between teacher and learner. It suggests that – despite the seemingly absolute nature of the curriculum – knowledge itself is a fluid, changing phenomenon, mediated by language, in which meanings continually change according to the political, social and economic forces which shape our society.

Chapter Two begins the children's stories with a short socio-historical introduction to the community into which they were born. It traces the journeys made by their grandfathers and fathers, pointing out how their mothers and grandmothers remained largely invisible through the years in which the community was becoming established in Bradford. It makes links between the development of the Pakistani-heritage community in Bradford and the growth of education in the city, focusing on some of the issues and events which have affected communication among the diverse groups in the city over the years, and still affect it today.

In Chapter Three, the home and community experiences of the children and the views of their parents about education are presented. Through examples of their talk, mostly taken from visits I made to their homes and conversations I had with their parents, I show some of the ways in which the children learn informally at home and in their community. This includes learning about distinctive aspects of their own cultures and languages; learning who they are and where they belong. Through quotations from conversations with their parents – particularly their mothers – I show some of their parents' concerns about their children's education.

Chapter Four traces the progress of the children at school as they move from Year Three to Year Six, making the transition from first to middle school in the process. It happened that, just as the children left Year Six, Bradford underwent a re-organisation which abolished the three-tier system which had been in place for about twenty years and replaced it with a two-tier one. Through examples of classroom talk, including teacher-teacher, teacher-child and child-child interaction, I illustrate different kinds of teaching and learning events. These show the active ways in which children mediate what is going on in the classroom, no matter what the pedagogy and content, and the ways in which successful learners can engage with and appropriate the classroom interaction for their own purposes.

In Chapter Five, I show another layer of interaction and some different perspectives on the issues which have been raised in Chapters Three and Four by presenting some of the teachers' viewpoints. Using extracts from conversations I had with teachers in first and middle schools, I illustrate some of the ways in which they view culture and the children's identities and ethnicities. Finally, I identify some of the problems they face in their work, some of the contradictions within which they are trying to operate.

The focus in Chapter Six is on the kinds of policies and practices which I believe can support children's learning in primary schools and promote a positive ethos in classrooms where all children will feel safe, valued and positive about themselves as learners. There are sections on supporting bilingualism, improving family involvement in children's learning, valuing and respecting what children bring to school and the implications of these for whole-school policies and for the individual primary teacher's professional identity and rôle.

Finally, Chapter Seven presents some strategies for promoting 'success in diversity' in primary classrooms through a focus on language. Two main themes are developed and explored: ways in which teachers can help children to use talk to enhance their learning and secondly, ways in which literature can be used as a resource for learning about language and culture and to promote a genuinely multicultural ethos. The chapter and the book end with some suggestions of resources which can make up a valuable and useful toolkit for teachers committed to helping their pupils succeed in diversity and become powerful, enthusiastic and independent learners as they progress through the education system.

1

THEORIES OF CULTURE, LANGUAGE AND LEARNING IN PRIMARY CLASSROOMS

It was a large, sunny room, cluttered with books and papers. Comfortable chairs surrounded a low central table, littered with everyday things – cups, plates, a candle on a saucer, a box of matches, a clock, piles of exercise books waiting to be marked. A little boy stood by the table, rummaging among the bits and pieces. His fingers found a small, hard, rectangular object. Curious, he picked it up. He held the heavy metallic bar in his hand and looked across with a slightly puzzled expression to where his mother was sitting. Then a man sitting on an armchair nearby leant over and dropped some paperclips onto the metal bar. They stuck to it. The little boy's expression turned to one of amazement. He gave a little shout of surprise. He pulled the paperclips off and felt the force that was compelling them to stick themselves back on again. By this time, he could hardly contain his astonishment, though it was now tinged with a little apprehension. The man gently took the paperclip-covered bar out of the child's hand and stuck it onto a metal lamp that was on the table. The little boy grabbed the bar, put it back on the lamp and took it off a few times, then tried to make it stick onto a china plate. Then he was off, running round the room, testing which things the bar would stick to and which it would not. He had a new game to play. He had also just been given a powerful learning experience.

This is a description of my son Moi's first encounter with a magnet. He was two or three years old at the time. The man who expertly constructed the experience was Mike, a secondary school science teacher of many years' standing. Mike was delighted by Moi's response and watched him with huge pleasure as he darted around the room, learning about magnetism. Mike commented on how, through watching Moi, he enjoyed the opportunity to re-discover the thrill of teaching a child something totally new. He talked about how, spending his time as he did in trying to get students through 'O' level and 'A' level exams, he often forgot how much teachers could learn from children about the pleasures of learning.

As teachers, we all need to keep reminding ourselves about the pleasures of learning. We need to spend time watching children and thinking about how they behave and respond to the world around them. This is one of the ways in which we develop our own theories of learning. These theories also develop from working with and talking to children, from reading what others have written about them and from analysing our own personal experiences of learning and being taught (not always the same thing). All these activities feed into our beliefs and attitudes about teaching and learning and our understanding of how, as teachers, we can best mediate learning for children – in other words, our theories.

The word 'theory' can be misunderstood. Its unconsidered use can create much stress and confusion in teaching. Theory is sometimes seen as something separate from practice, dreamt up by theorists who – many teachers suspect – don't know much about the realities of classroom life. Theory has come to be regarded by some as irrelevant or as unnecessarily complicated, separate from and even getting in the way of good practice. But this should not be so. Teaching is essentially a practical activity, and can be physically exhausting – as all teachers know. It is also a delicate, subtle set of processes, which need to be informed, guided and adapted by appropriate theory. Woods (1996) called teaching an 'art', and described it as 'expressive and emergent, intuitive and flexible, spontaneous and emotional'. As teachers, we are not (or should not be) unthinking robots, programmed to follow sets of instructions in totally predictable and unchanging ways. We are individuals, and also members of social and cultural groups. We have our own experiences, beliefs, knowledge, attitudes and preferences. All of these contribute to our theories which we bring to the job of teaching the children or students in our care.

Theory is an essential aspect of the enterprise of teaching. It is needed to inform and underpin our practice. Otherwise we risk becoming those unthinking, programmed robots that we know would be so harmful in the classroom. All teachers have – sometimes intuitively or even unknowingly – theories of learning. Without them, they couldn't decide how to teach. For some, the theories are hidden, buried beneath their actions. It can enormously improve your teaching if you try to dig out your precise theories of learning. The kinds of theories we need to help us become excellent teachers are those that develop from our practice and also develop along with it, constantly feeding back into it. When I did my teacher training, I don't think I listened very hard to the lecturers who told us about educational theories. I was too preoccupied with thinking about how I was going to control the class on my next teaching practice, and what I was going to teach them. After I had been teaching for some time, I did other courses and was faced again with books to read and topics to discuss in seminars. It was then I realised that the reading, thinking and talking – and even the writing of essays – are all important aspects of developing all the skills required of a teacher.

What matters about theory and practice is their interaction – each needs to arise from and be fed and developed by the other. One without the other is sterile. This dynamic relationship – sometimes called praxis – describes how I want to present my ideas about culture, language and learning in this book. In this first chapter, I want to explain my own theories. These have been formed from my own practical experience with children both outside and inside classrooms as well as from reading, talking and writing about how teaching and learning take place in primary classrooms. This will provide a context for the chapters that follow. There are six main sections in this introductory chapter:

- *Cultures and learning*, where I explain how I see teaching and learning as culturally and socially based activities

- *Language and learning*, where I discuss the rôle which I think language plays in learning, both before children begin school and as they become pupils in mainstream classrooms

- *Learning the language*, where I argue that in order to succeed in school, children need to become experts at using specific and specialised forms of language

- *What counts as knowledge*, where I discuss how the knowledge that is important in school is often different from the kinds of things children know and learn in their out-of-school lives

- *Languages for success in learning*, where I focus on the rôle of talk in learning, and also the ways in which bilingualism can influence children's opportunities in school

- *Cultures of learning and being yourself*, where I draw the threads of my argument together and show what I mean by classroom cultures which enable children to succeed

Each section weaves together stories from my personal and professional experience, and the ideas I have gained from reading about the issues. Together, they spell out what I regard as the main factors which underpin successful learning in primary schools. My focus is on ethnically diverse classrooms as that is where I have gained all my experience, but I believe that the ideas are equally valid for all primary classrooms.

Cultures and learning

Spend a little time watching and listening in a typical primary classroom, and you will quickly gain a sense that what is happening is very complex. A wide diversity of events are taking place. A vast amount of interaction and negotiation is going on. Much of the activity is directed by the teacher or other adults, but a significant amount is controlled by the children, some of it outside the teacher's notice. In all that is happening, talk is a crucial element, sometimes the focus of the negotiation and at times the evidence for what has been learnt. It is obvious that learning is not a smooth, easy business of one-way transmission. In order to help to explain what is happening and why, the most helpful model of learning I have come across is the socio-cultural one most commonly associated with Vygotsky (1978, 1986). It goes furthest to explain the realities of primary classrooms as I have experienced them. It suggests that learning is strongly socially situated in specific contexts and develops from and within the relationships between teachers and learners. It also suggests that language – predominantly talk – is an important element of these contexts and relationships. In socio-cultural models, teacher-pupil and pupil-pupil interaction are seen as key elements in the processes of teaching and learning.

As well as showing the importance of talking for learning, Vygotsky's ideas help us to recognise the essential links between learning and culture. Through this, they can help to identify the factors which enable individual learners to succeed, or cause them to fail, in their learning. Sonia Nieto (1999), in her book about 'creating multicultural learning communities', uses Vygotsky's model to develop her own ideas about the kinds of learning that best support children from ethnic minorities in mainstream classrooms. She also makes the point that such a model, based as it is on sound general principles, supports learning for all children. Nieto develops her ideas as a set of five statements which – she suggests – should underpin children's learning at all levels. These are:

- Learning is actively constructed
- Learning grows from and builds on the learner's prior experiences
- Learning is influenced by cultural differences
- Learning is influenced by the context in which it occurs
- Learning is socially mediated, and develops within a culture and a community

---

The word 'culture' is important here, and needs some clarification. It has many different definitions. Nieto defines culture very much in terms of what people do in their daily lives, inevitably influenced by historical, economic and political factors. She identifies seven attributes of culture, which together reflect its fluid nature and also its significance in children's learning experiences. For Nieto, culture is:

- dynamic
- multifaceted
- embedded in contexts
- influenced by social, economic and political factors
- socially constructed
- learned (ie it is not innate)
- dialectical

Street (1993) sums up its dynamic, active, changing qualities by suggesting that culture is 'a verb' and not a noun, a process rather than a product. Nieto goes on to suggest that the Vygotskyan perspective provides us with 'a hopeful framework' for thinking about learning. If successful learning is not just a matter for the individual learner but is a result of the culturally constructed dialogues between teachers and learner, then surely – Nieto argues – conditions can be created in schools that can help most children to learn.

Learning, to use Margaret Donaldson's (1978) evocative word, is 'embedded' in the learner's culture, their experiences of the world and of themselves as an individual and social being within it. For young children, learning is physical and multi-sensory. They use whatever comes to hand (literally, in many cases) as tools to help them to learn. Language becomes one of those tools, but it is only one of many. The focus is on exploring the world around them, finding out, discovering what things mean. I remember one day a visitor from England to our house in Sierra Leone expressing anxiety when she saw my daughter at play. Feimatta, aged three, was busy 'helping' Betty our cook to prepare the mid-day meal, along with Betty's daughter, Tiangé, also three. The two little girls had made a small fire next to Betty's large one, and were busily chopping up leaves and twigs which they had collected. They dropped their 'vegetables' into an old tin can with a splash of muddy water, placed it on their fire and took turns to stir it round with a stick. Most young children brought up in England are kept away from fire, sharp knives and old tin cans. Most young children in Sierra Leone learn to play with these potentially dangerous things safely, usually in the context of work alongside an adult. For both sets of children, the cultural practices and the physical settings which surround them provide the contexts for learning.

When Feimatta and her brother began attending school in England at the ages of seven and ten, their teachers were highly impressed with their reading attainment and knowledge of the times tables. In Sierra Leone, we had had no television, so we spent most evenings reading. The children had practised their times tables in school almost daily from the age of four. The only concern Feimatta's teacher in England had was that she found it difficult to use equipment in the classroom such as the large plastic weighing scales. She had never seen anything like them before, let alone handled them. She told me that she didn't realise what the teacher meant when she asked her to balance them.

Barbara Rogoff's fascinating book *Apprenticeship in Thinking* (1990) provides many examples of context-based, cultural learning from a wide range of settings, and also a discussion of the implications for mainstream education. Barry Hine's novel *A Kestrel for a Knave* (1968), superbly filmed a year later as *Kes*, covers the same ground. Billy Casper, a 'failure' in his secondary modern school, had expert knowledge of wild birds which he had acquired for himself because of his fascination with them. He kept and trained his own kestrel and spent hours with it. None of his teachers knew anything about this until one day his English teacher offered him the space in a lesson to share his knowledge. Billy's eloquence when talking about his kestrel showed how right the teacher was to do this.

Language and learning

As well as the physical, multi-sensory kind of learning which – obviously – continues beyond the early stages, our 'embedded' learning includes language in the forms of both oracy and literacy. Again, young children start with what is most important to them. The most pressing things they want to learn are all about what things are, what they can do, and what their significance is to them. Their awareness of written forms grows from this and then feeds back into it. It will probably come as no surprise in our globalised world to hear that the most commonly identified written word for three-year olds anywhere it has been tested the world over is 'McDonalds'. The twin golden arches are often enough for children to be able to read the whole word. It's what it means for them that counts: something nice to eat or a toy or maybe even a party. When they do get to school, their meanings for the word grow. Many five-year old children in England, thanks to their daily doses of the Literacy Hour, could tell you that it begins with a blend of three consonants and contains two short vowel sounds ... and perhaps more besides.

The McDonalds example shows the power of language to transcend spatial and cultural distances. In terms of children's learning, it is also important to recognise the ways in which language defines cultural, spatial and social boundaries and so can narrow down our worlds. Shirley Brice Heath's *Ways with Words* (1983) was perhaps the first large study of the ways in which ethnically and socially diverse communities living side by side used language. Heath provides many rich examples of the ways in which members of 'poor white', 'middle class white' and 'poor black' communities in the same region of southeastern USA talked with others within their groups. She shows how each group constructed their cultural contexts very differently and taught their children about what it meant to belong in their respective communities. In this way, she argues, they passed on to their children an awareness and understanding of how language is used to communicate meanings and messages. Thus, Heath argued, did each community construct a distinctive social identity, ways of belonging to and being part of a social group and of understanding and responding to others. In other words – in Nieto's terms – a culture.

So when the children Heath studied began school, they went there with a ready-formed sense of how they should behave as part of a group. The ways in which they used language both defined and were defined by this sense. For many, the ways their teachers used language were new and strange. Their teachers, like the rest of us, could cue into and sympathise best with those children whose 'ways with words' most closely resembled their own. Their expectations of the children were inevitably influenced by their judgements of the different ways the children used language. The consequences of such judgements for assessing children's attainment and potential have been well documented in various settings. Children's success in school often hangs in this balance right from the start. External judgements, often vital for children's future educational and employment opportunities, usually do little more than confirm these initial judgements.

In primary classrooms, then, a great deal of negotiation, mostly through talk, needs to take place between teachers and learners. When the participants in classrooms have differing language and cultural backgrounds, this adds to the complexity and the risks of misunderstanding, as Heath's research shows. But in some sense all children need to learn a new language when they begin school. The main business going on in the classroom may be about gaining knowledge, but this does not take place in a vacuum. The new language that has to be learnt is all about the culture of the classroom in which the children are learning. It is about the ways they are expected to behave as individuals and to relate to others, as well as the knowledge they are expected to learn. There are three big questions about education which this new classroom language is helping the children to form their own answers to:

- *What* are we learning?
- *How* are we learning it?
- *Why* are we learning it?

These can be regarded as the main elements of the culture of the classroom. For children, the knowledge to be learnt is strongly contextualised in the ways they are expected to behave. The title of Mary Willes' book *Children into Pupils* (1983) neatly sums up what this means for children in terms of their identities and their self-awareness as they move through school.

Someone once told me a story which illustrates this nicely. It is about an OFSTED Inspector who had the tables neatly turned on him. As he sat at the back of the class, quietly observing what was going on, a child approached him. The conversation went something like this:

Child:	What are you doing?
Inspector:	Writing.
Child:	Can you do fullstops and capital letters?
Inspector:	Yes.
Child:	(pointing to another part of the classroom) Well, you should be sitting over there, then.

The story is probably apocryphal but it shows what I mean about children learning the culture along with the knowledge in the classroom; the how and why along with the what.

Learning the language

In school, children need to learn how to do a great many new things with language that they have most probably never done before, and may never do anywhere else but in the classroom. As they progress through school, the language they need to do these things becomes more and more self-referential and specific. Donaldson (1978) talks about how, as they move through school, children have to progress from learning which is strongly 'embedded' in the surrounding contexts to learning which is 'disembedded' and thus much more dependent on the language in which it is framed. This involves learning to use new kinds of language in new kinds of ways to perform new kinds of tasks. Many of these activities are special to classrooms, demanding of learners ways of understanding and responding through language that they do not have to use in any other parts of their lives. For example, they have to learn to write answers to questions, rather than say them (and usually 'in complete sentences'), to fill in blanks, to write instructions for other people, to report on things they have done, to summarise ideas from texts, to write lists of correctly-spelt words ... the list goes on. In order to succeed in school, children have to learn to talk, read and write in specific and specialised ways. And it doesn't end there. To show that they have done this successfully, children have then to pass tests at certain points in their school careers, which require them to display this highly specialised knowledge.

These tests, SATs in primary schools, require children to do all kinds of things. Here is an example of a SATs task in mathematics for seven-year olds. The question is about the number of buses needed to take a large group of children on a journey:

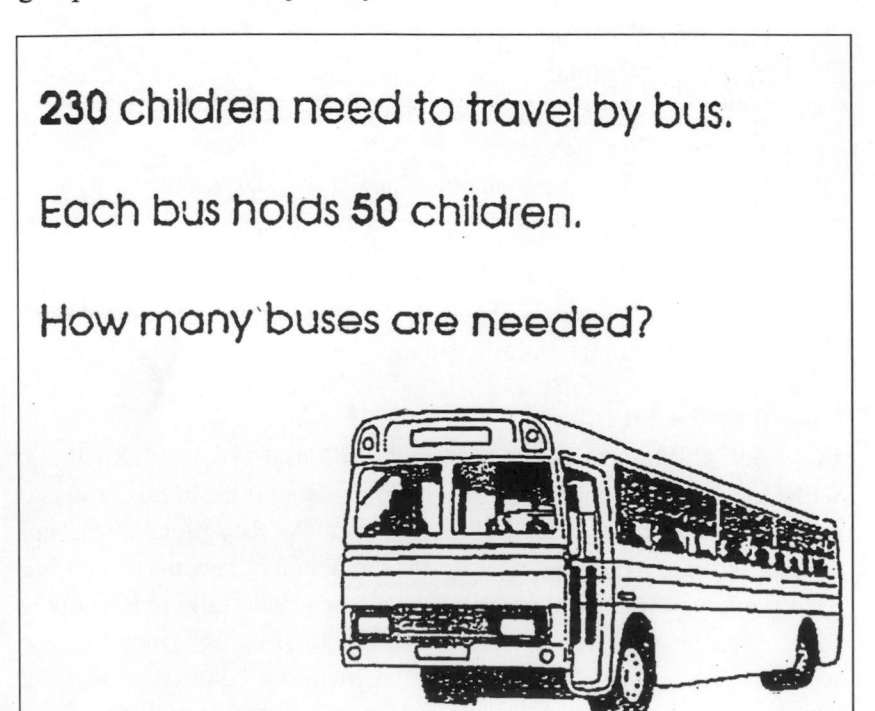

230 children need to travel by bus.

Each bus holds **50** children.

How many buses are needed?

No one in the real world would ever need to perform a task like this. If they wanted buses to go on a journey, they would count how many children were going – and they wouldn't forget the adults, as the question seems to do. Then they would 'phone the bus company, tell them where they wanted to go, how many people were going and ask them to arrange it. But we all know that what is shown here is not about real buses and real children going on a real journey. It is about something altogether different. We know what it is about, and how to go about doing what is required. QCA, who set the SATs, provide us with a mark scheme so that we can check that we have done the right thing. We also know why we need to do it in the way that the mark scheme expects – in order to pass the test. But not all children have fully learnt the how and why of this kind of thing at the age of seven. Here is how one child responded to the question:

230 children need to travel by bus.

Each bus holds **50** children.

How many buses are needed? 4 and ½ little bus that carries 30.

If you count all the little marks in the buses, you will find that there are, indeed, 230. This child clearly knows quite a lot of maths. He also understands about the business of getting children onto buses. He has found a way to work out the number of buses needed for a journey with a large number of children. He's clearly got a great future ahead of him as a tour organiser. But from the evidence here, he hasn't learnt yet how you pass SATs tests. He doesn't yet seem to have learnt that trick you need in Maths tests of disembedding the task you have to do from the surrounding contexts. When the test marker saw this child's answer, he didn't know what to do. Nowhere on his paper had the child written the number 5, which was the correct answer to the question given on the mark scheme. The child's response generated much discussion between markers and examiners. The story ended happily – the child was given his mark for the question, and he got the expected level on the test. But no one was able to give him the credit he deserved for his drawings of buses or the originality of his thinking.

What counts as knowledge

'Miss, you've got a new car.'

Asif's greeting to me as I arrived at school that morning contained a note of satisfaction. I had been working at the school for about a year, and had driven my ancient Renault into the playground every morning and parked it alongside the other teachers' cars. But for the first time, on that particular morning, I had arrived in the shiny (almost) new Volvo which I'd just traded the Renault in for. Asif, in Year Six, had spotted this immediately and wanted to discuss my upgraded car ownership in serious terms. He continued with his evaluation of my smart new vehicle, 'It's good, Miss. Much better than that old car. GL's a good car for a teacher.' I felt suitably affirmed in my choice. He went on, 'Miss, why didn't you get one with a spoiler? They go much better with a spoiler.' Not being totally sure what a spoiler was, I nodded cautiously and suggested to Asif that he go to his classroom for registration.

Like many ten-year old boys, Asif had an encyclopaedic knowledge about cars and acute powers of observation where they were concerned. Cars mattered to him in a way that they have never really mattered to me. His knowledge was more than factual. He had clear views about what cars represented economically and socially, who should own and drive which models. His dad, made unemployed by the closure of the textile mills, was a taxi driver. Perhaps Asif himself is a taxi driver now too. But because his knowledge of the Vikings – the cross-curricular topic we were doing in Year Six that half term – was not as good and his interest and sense of personal investment in them not as strong, Asif was having a bad time in the classroom. He tended to cover this up by disrupting the lessons. He had no power to decide what counted as knowledge in that classroom. That power lay elsewhere. Commentators such as Apple (1982, 1993) remind us of how 'knowledge' is a constantly changing phenomenon, shaped in the 'ideological, political and economic spheres of society'. There is nothing neutral about it. Apple makes explicit the connections between knowledge and power and shows how the curriculum is one of the most lively battle sites between them. Through centrally developed and imposed curricula, national governments establish the knowledge that counts – and that which doesn't count for success within their domains.

If we look at school curricula historically, we see clearly the political, social and economic imperatives which underpin their formation. The Bradford School Board, set up in 1870, was by all accounts a dynamic body which did much to develop the causes of education in the city, as the next chapter recounts. Here is part of the regulations they devised for what should be taught in the magnificent board schools they built. This is what they prescribed as the curriculum for Boys' and Girls' Departments in the 1870s:

---

(1) Bible and Principles of Religion and Morality

(2) Reading, Writing and Arithmetic, Singing and Drill, English Grammar, Composition, Writing from Dictation, Systemised Object lesson and Elementary Physiology and Science, English History, Elementary geography, Elementary Drawing, Social Economy.

Principles of Book-keeping (in boys' departments)

Plain Needlework, Cutting Out and Domestic Economy (in girls' departments)

(City of Bradford Corporation, 1970)

The future workers in the thriving textile industry in Bradford were clearly being well prepared to take on their allotted, gendered and class-determined rôles in keeping that industry going.

Ross (2000) describes and analyses the processes of curriculum selection and design which led to the construction of the English National Curriculum in its various incarnations. He argues that by the time Curriculum 2000 was in the making, the forces that controlled these processes were essentially backward looking and fearful of progress. He suggests that they sought to use the curriculum as a means 'to invent a new form of national identity', one that was anxious about difference and diversity. So the curriculum aimed to promote a model of uniformity and cultural cohesion in defining a 'common culture' for all members of English society. Former head of SCAA – later QCA – Nicholas Tate's (1996) 'four big ideas' about the curriculum's rôle in the transmission of culture sum up these anxieties with their insistence on a narrow vision of British culture, history, literature, art and music. Such influences on the construction of a national curriculum do not bode well for the success of children such as Asif.

The knowledge that counts in school is what the powers that be decide it should be. Language has a major part to play in how this knowledge is constructed and packaged. Our department at college ran projects for several years in which we worked alongside teacher trainers and students from Poland. I remember once having a long conversation with a visiting professor about science education. He confessed, quite genuinely, that he was puzzled about what science education was. When he had first read the term in a document written by science colleagues in the department, he understood the word 'science' in terms of its broader definition of 'knowledge' rather than as a specific curriculum subject. This is what the Polish language equivalent relates more closely to, as does the etymological derivation of the word. He did not grasp immediately that it referred to the branch of knowledge usually known as the natural sciences, which is how the word is now normally used in educational discourse in England. Its meaning has been narrowed down.

In similar vein, Ross (2000) talks about the shift in the status of the category of knowledge labelled as Science on the school curriculum. It had little recognition as a valid school subject at the end of the nineteenth century, being regarded as of lower status than other branches of knowledge such as grammar. It is interesting to see it on the Bradford School Board list. Perhaps the trustees felt it to be an appropriate part of the required knowledge of future mill workers. By the end of the twentieth century, according to Ross, Science had come to be regarded as 'an essential element of the well-educated person' and to have a central place on the school curriculum.

The ways we use words, then, reflect the ways we construct our knowledge of the world. Meanings change to reflect changes in cultural and social practices. One summer's day, about eight years ago, I was driving into town with my son, then aged about sixteen. We passed the following advertisement on a hoarding by the side of the road:

I smiled to myself at the cleverness of the advertisers and their targeting of financially stretched forty-somethings with their memories of the seventies and freewheeling Simon and Garfunkel songs. Moi stared intently out of the car window. Then he turned to me and asked, 'What does groovy mean?'

The meanings of words, and so the knowledge they represent, can also be dangerously manipulated for more overtly political purposes. Orwellian doublespeak is not such a far-fetched notion. On March 25, 1999, on my way to work at college, I passed a newspaper billboard which announced the following headline:

ALLIES BLITZ SERBIA

The NATO bombings of Belgrade had started that morning in an attempt to oust Milosevic from Serbia. I had just been listening at home to reports on the *Today* programme about Serbs demonstrating in London against the attacks. These were followed by an interview with an elderly Serbian gentleman. He talked about how his family had hidden a British airman shot down in 1941 and how they felt they were making a great sacrifice to defend Europe against the Nazis. He admitted he wasn't sure any more in 1999 if his country was part of Europe. It made me realise how the meanings of each of the three words in that headline had changed, some of them more than once, over the past sixty years as a consequence of the political, economic and social forces which shaped major historical events in the twentieth century.

Words are often used to label highly contested ideas and actions. But in the act of labelling, the unstable, fluid qualities of those ideas sometimes get forgotten. What counts as knowledge is not a neutral, straightforward matter. As with the three words in the headline, it is often highly political. Children need to be helped to recognise this and to learn how to analyse the ways in which language can be used to either close down or open out our understandings of the politics of knowledge. One of the best ways we can do this as teachers is to talk about such ideas with our pupils, and help develop their skills as critical readers, watchers and listeners. Through our conversations with them, we need to aim to develop their critical awareness of ways in which language is a valuable tool for understanding and explaining the world. But it is a dangerous tool. If its power is not recognised, it can become a weapon to attack the weak and powerless.

Languages for success in learning

The rôle of talk in successful learning should not be underestimated. There is a great deal of research which demonstrates the importance of collaborative talk for all – not just multilingual – children's learning. Projects like the National Oracy Project (Norman, 1992) showed how talk contributes to effective learning in a vast range of ways. There are many studies of classroom interaction which show how talk is an essential aspect of learning. One that I have found especially illuminating in understanding the specific ways in which talk can support cognitive development is *Constructing Knowledge Together*. Here Wells and Chang-Wells (1992) provide examples of talk from multilingual classrooms which offers children the opportunity for 'collaborative sense-making' with their peers. They argue that talk is 'the very essence of educational activity'. They emphasise the value of collaborative talk for 'literate thinking' which they define as thought which:

> ... exploits the symbolic potential of language to enable the thought processes themselves to become the objects of thought...

According to Wells and Chang-Wells, 'literate thinkers' are able to 'exploit the symbolic potential of external representation as an aid to the construction of inner meaning', whether in speech or writing. In other words, talk develops thinking which underpins literacy, the main route to learning in our education system.

In numerous classrooms, in many different ways, collaborative talk is thus 'a means for people to think and learn together' (Mercer, 1995). The word 'together' is important. Talk needs to be part of the way children learn in classrooms as well as something to be learnt in itself. This means their learning needs to be active and dialogic. Not only do children need to *learn to talk*, they also need to *talk to learn* and this is true across the whole curriculum. Learning takes place in and through the interaction and negotiation which talk allows. Teachers and learners need to negotiate and construct mutually supporting contexts in order for this to happen.

If we add the dimensions of diversity and multilingualism to the classroom negotiation, another layer of complexity is created. Many children in Britain (and proportionately many more in the world as a whole) bring to their classrooms languages and varieties of language that their classmates and teachers may not share. These all add to the context – whether in positive or negative ways depends to a large extent on what the participants believe about them. Language diversity can be seen as a positive or a negative aspect of classroom contexts.

This lesson was reinforced for me by my experiences of teaching and learning in Africa. In the places where I worked, multilingualism was just another part of people's lives. Children regularly spoke several languages at home. Then they went to school and learnt English as another one which they needed for different reasons and purposes. It didn't supplant or replace those they already possessed. It was simply added to them. My own children, born in Sierra Leone, both spoke three languages at the age of three – they have forgotten two of them since. They knew which language to speak to any visitor who came to the house, and would happily do so. It was just part of their experience. After my daughter had spent her first day in an English primary classroom at the age of seven, she came home and expressed surprise that the other children in her class 'didn't speak any languages'.

Despite the overwhelming evidence for the positive cognitive effects of bilingualism (Cummins, 1996, provides an excellent summary), it is still largely perceived as a problem in many mainstream classrooms in England. This attitude is in large part a reflection of the power relationships between the bilingual communities themselves and the wider society. In privileged socio-economic communities, *additive* bilingualism is valued and seen as an asset as long as the languages concerned have the right status. Cummins' own work with French-English bilinguals in Canada illustrates this. But towards groups with low socioeconomic status whose community languages have no cultural capital in the society in which they are living, attitudes are different. For them, the pressure in school is to learn English as quickly as possible in order to get on economically and socially. The outcome of this is often a *subtractive* bilingualism, which has negative cognitive effects. Thus teachers' low expectations of such bilingual children are reinforced. As Cummins (1996 and 2000) shows, such outcomes are harmful to the self-confidence and identities of individual learners and of the community as a whole.

Similar negative effects can arise from attitudes to dialect and accent diversity as well as to different languages. Some of my first teaching experiences were as a student in Aberdeen in the 1970s. My shaky confidence was strongly affected by my problems in understanding the accents of the children I was supposed to be teaching. In this case, I was the ethnic minority, being English in a Scottish setting, and at a time when there was some hostility towards the English companies who were perceived as stealing 'Scotland's oil' from the North Sea. In one classroom, the children, partly influenced by their teacher, definitely saw me as an outsider. They didn't want me to understand what they were saying and they made sure I didn't. In another, the children took a more positive attitude to my Englishness and invited me to share their own distinctive variety of English. This taught me very effectively that it wasn't so much the language itself that was the issue, but the attitudes of the speakers and listeners and the relationships between them.

At the same time as my own children were finding out what it meant to be learners in English classrooms, I was finding out again what it was like to be a teacher. The school where I was working had a high proportion of bilingual children. They were mostly of Pakistani heritage, but they reminded me strongly of the children I had taught in Sierra Leone. They were alert and lively, interested in and knowledgeable about the world around them, and very aware of and interested in languages. When I got to know them, they would discuss their home cultures perceptively, showing their sophisticated awareness of language and cultural diversity. Several of them spotted immediately that my accent was different from other staff because I was not from the local area. They noticed that there were specific words which I pronounced differently. They even noticed that my accent was similar to that of another teacher in the school, who turned out to come from the same part of the country as I did. This led to all kinds of discussions about accent, dialect and language diversity.

These discussions usually took place in the spaces between the formal lessons at lunchtimes or playtimes. When they were in their classrooms, the children were often much more silent. They were discouraged from using their home languages. Many of the teachers felt strongly that this was the only way they would learn English. The result was that the children had tacitly learnt that it was inappropriate and unacceptable to speak or write any language but English in school. This effectively closed down their opportunities to learn, as many of them had relatively low proficiency in spoken and written English compared with their home languages and could not really express what they wanted to say. They were, in effect, experiencing the subtractive bilingualism that Cummins describes. This was no doubt a contributory factor to the fact that they did not make much academic progress in the four years they spent in the school. Measured standards in most curriculum subjects were low. 'Their' problems were the cause for much genuine concern on the part of the teachers in the school and the LEA advisory service. Much effort was spent in trying to think of ways to make up for 'their' deficits. But no matter what was tried, results remained poor, the school languished at the lower end of the league tables. Such evidence can be taken to 'prove' that the children were in some way academically deficient. But it could also, surely, indicate that what they did know was not being taken into account.

Cultures of learning and being yourself

A few years ago, I took a group of student teachers to Islamabad in Pakistan. They did some teaching practice in English medium primary schools. I was amazed by the differences I observed in the organisation and ambience of the classrooms when compared to the schools I knew in Yorkshire. In Islamabad, children from the age of six or seven sat at desks in rows in classrooms almost devoid of wall displays or resources. They copied down notes from the blackboard and read aloud from their textbooks after the teacher. They produced pages of neat handwriting and correct exercises in English spelling, grammar and punctuation. Their concentration appeared limitless. Classroom discipline was impeccable. In Yorkshire, in bright, comparatively well-resourced classrooms, teachers find that children of Pakistani heritage of the same age cannot sit still for more than five minutes at a time. They find that the children cannot listen to instructions. They worry about offering them work which might be too demanding or fail to hold their interest.

These differences seem to reflect polarised views about what makes an effective learning environment. By effective, I do not mean better in any absolute sense. I am not seeking to compare or make value judgements about the different models of learning represented in the classrooms. What interests me is the immense difference in the classroom cultures of the two settings. They reflect vastly different assumptions about what teachers do and what learners do, and how the two groups of key players in the game of school understand each other's actions. In the Pakistani primary classrooms I visited, the effectiveness seemed to come about because the teacher (usually a woman) and her pupils had clear shared understandings about how things should be done. They trusted each other and knew what to expect of each other. These expectations might, to a 'western' observer, be based on dubious pedagogic principles, but that does not matter. The participants' belief in their effectiveness made them work in the way that everyone expected. In contrast, in many ethnically diverse classrooms in Britain, both teachers and pupils appear to be confused about what is going on. The teachers are struggling to implement a curriculum which they do not control and which does not seem to fit into the contexts in which they are working. The children often do not appear to recognise as 'teaching' the events that are taking place and are not sure what is expected of them as pupils.

The complexity is greater for the children who also attend community school in the evenings or at the weekend, where they are learning to read and write a different script. There is much evidence that biliteracy has cognitive advantages, and some of the children's conversations quoted in Chapter Three (especially pages 46-47) demonstrate this. Nevertheless, it is still the case that literacy in Urdu, Bengali or other languages is not regarded by most mainstream teachers as a positive asset – though literacy in French or German usually is. Teachers in mainstream schools worry about the negative consequences for children of spending time in the community schools when they should be practising their English. At the same time, teachers in the community schools worry about the seeming informality of learning in mainstream schools and its effects on the children's general behaviour. The children, as usual, are caught in the middle. What could potentially be a positive learning experience is turned into a problem. Both sets of teachers have the children's interests at heart, but what is needed is the opportunity for a dialogue in which the strengths of the different approaches can be recognised. This issue is discussed further in Chapter Six.

The contrasts I noticed between schools in Pakistan and Britain helped to shape my theories about the issues which need to be considered when trying to work out what creates 'successful' learning contexts. It is certainly essential to provide appropriate content, to think about classroom organisation and resources designed for the level and experience of the learners. But these are like the building blocks of the house which have nothing in themselves to hold them together and give them shape. What can hold them together is the shared culture between teachers and learners, the medium within which all participants can recognise and feel comfortable about what is taking place. The active participation of the learners is crucial. More than ever, I have come to recognise that teaching cannot be a process of transferring knowledge from the teacher to the taught unless the taught agree for it to be so.

One of the assignments we set our students as they begin their four-year BA QTS course to become primary teachers is to write an autobiographical piece. They often choose to write about themselves as learners. One of the first pieces I ever received moved me powerfully, and still does. Its title was *I want to be someone else*. The writer, Rukhsana, has now been an excellent teacher for several years. I'm sure that the experience she wrote about is still an important motivation for her teaching, the feelings she so vividly described still buried somewhere deep inside her. She wrote about herself as a young child, beginning school in England unable to speak English. No one else in the class could speak Punjabi, so she had no one to talk to. A few weeks later, another little girl arrived who could speak Punjabi and also some English. Life improved considerably for Rukhsana. But a while later something happened which affected her profoundly. One day, she was happily working with her bilingual friend when the teacher appeared in front of her, holding up a colourful object and saying something to her. Rukhsana did not understand the words, but knew that something was expected of her. Her friend explained to her in Punjabi that the teacher wanted her to name the colour of the object. But, before she could reply, the teacher told her interpreter off in no uncertain terms and sent her away to the other side of the classroom. Rukhsana continues her story:

> The teacher left me staring blankly at the other children. Every one of them was doing something: playing, reading, working or talking in English. I sat back and felt sorry for myself. The teacher had gone on to assessing other children as if nothing dramatic had really happened. Probably thinking, just an incident with an Asian child who does nor know colours or anything else for that matter. This was a day that I felt so many emotions inside me. Feelings that I had never experienced before. I did not want to be myself.

To try to understand the ways in which children who do not share the languages and cultures of their teachers can succeed as learners, it can be helpful to imagine their experiences and knowledge as overlapping layers in concentric circles, with themselves as individuals in the centre. They experience language, culture and knowledge in interaction with others within and across each layer, something like the diagram opposite:

The child in the centre is influenced in different ways by interaction with each outer layer. In order to understand how children succeed as learners, we need to unpeel the layers without destroying the core. When the languages and cultures of the home are not the ones that have

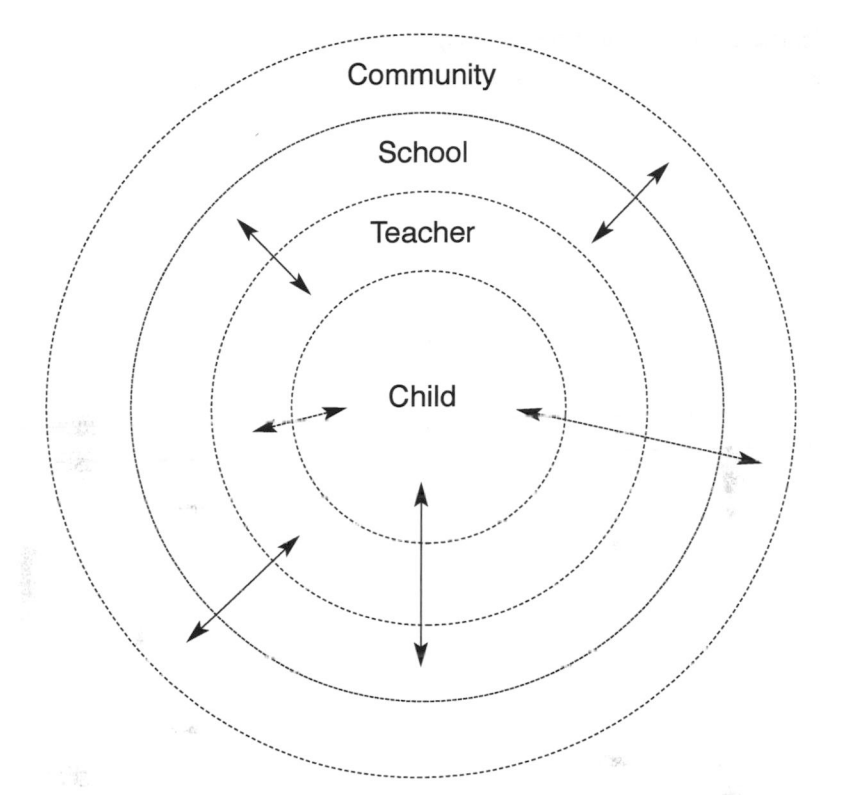

a central place in the classroom, we as teachers cannot deny that they are there or assume that they are not significant. If we did, we would be denying the children who own them the opportunity to be themselves.

We all have our own personal and communal cultures, our public and private identities. We all succeed best at what we are doing when we feel that our private and personal selves are accepted *within* the larger public spheres that we inhabit and are not separated and dislocated from them. We all have to begin with being ourselves. In the chapters that follow, I provide evidence from the different layers of experience about the language, learning and cultural experiences of a small group of successful bilingual learners as they move through Key Stage Two. On the way, I point out some of the factors which helped them to succeed and which could, perhaps, be used to help all learners in their different contexts to do the same.

SUMMARY OF KEY ISSUES

In this chapter, I have discussed the rôle of theory for teachers in effective teaching and learning and set out some of the theories which for me underpin successful teaching in ethnically diverse classrooms. These are all to do with issues of language, culture and learning, and the key points can be set out as follows:

- There are different ways of theorising learning, and these theories are continually evolving

- Teachers need to work out their own theories which underpin their practice – doing so will help them to improve their practice and develop as teachers

- The Vygotskyan model is helpful, presenting learning as a socio-cultural process which is dependent on context and on the interaction between teachers and learners

- Knowledge is not fixed and unchanging but is, on the contrary, developed and changed by social, political and economic forces

- Children's learning is strongly influenced by factors outside the classroom as well as those inside it

- The most effective teaching and learning happens when teachers and learners share values and views about how it should be done, when teachers can see things through their learners' eyes and understand their viewpoints

- We cannot deny the significance of children's home language and cultural experiences when they come to school.

2

SETTING THE SCENE: THE HISTORY OF DIVERSITY IN BRADFORD – STARTING POINTS FOR RESEARCH

Seeking better lives

> ... at once one of the most provincial and yet one of the most cosmopolitan of English provincial cities ... Bradford was determinedly Yorkshire and provincial but some of its suburbs reached as far as Frankfurt or Leipzig.

So wrote J. B. Priestley, a native of Bradford, in 1895. He captures both the rich diversity and the contrariness of his home town. He was writing at the end of a century in which Bradford had grown rapidly as a centre for textile manufacturing and for international trade. In 1801 there was one textile mill in the town; by 1851 there were 130. Bradford woollens had become famous all over the world. They were proudly displayed in the Great Exhibition in Crystal Palace in 1851. In 1864, the Wool Exchange was built in the centre of the town, epitomising Bradford's importance for international commerce. For a time, world prices for wool were set and global trade was regulated there. Today the building houses the largest bookshop in the city. Statues of Cobden, Bright and other champions of free trade still preside on their pedestals over the bookshelf browsers and the patrons of the coffee shop.

These twin strands of progress – industry and commerce – have attracted different groups of immigrants to Bradford from the beginning of the nineteenth century. Irish families arrived, escaping the extreme poverty and deprivation of their homeland. Many of them walked from the Liverpool docks pulling all their worldly belongings in carts. They were among the first generation of labourers to work in the large new mills. At about the same time, wealthy traders, mostly of Jewish origin, began arriving from Germany and establishing a warehouse district near the centre of the town, in an area still known as Little Germany. They kept the wheels of enterprise turning, quickly founding a Chamber of Commerce to regulate their business. And just as quickly, they took themselves away from the noise and squalor of the town centre to newly built mansions on the salubrious slopes of the surrounding hills. They were a powerful influence on the cultural life and the development of education in the town. Bradford elected its first Jewish mayor in 1864 .

Business continued to thrive and the new arrivals kept coming. As well as from Germany and Ireland, people came to Bradford from Poland, the Ukraine, Latvia, Estonia, Bielorussia, Yugoslavia, Lithuania, Italy, Greece, Cyprus and the Caribbean (Halstead, 1988). Just before the Second World War, men from South Asia began arriving in Bradford and other cities in West Yorkshire. The first were seamen, originally from India. They arrived in England at the ports of Hull, Liverpool and Middlesbrough and were directed inland to find work in Yorkshire in the textile mills and munitions factories which were to supply the war effort. They were welcome and had much to contribute. In the 1950s, men from the Mirpur and Azad Kashmir regions of the new nation of Pakistan increased the number of South Asian recruits to the workforce, often joining fathers, uncles, brothers and cousins who had gone before them. To a lesser extent, men came also from India and – later – from the new nation of Bangladesh. In many ways they were, as Singh (1994) points out, continuing the long traditions of migration from their home-lands to seek a better life elsewhere. One of the earliest arrivals in Bradford from South Asia describes his own journey:

> I came over here in 1938. It was a village tradition, go out and earn some money. In the village there was no other job besides helping your parents on the farm, so I thought of going abroad. I had an uncle over here, I had correspondence with him, he was to help me over here ... (see Singh, 1994)

Other factors influenced the migration. Many of the Pakistani men who came from Mirpur in the 1950s had sacrificed their farmland and sometimes their whole villages to the building of the Mangla Dam by the British government. The compensation money they received funded their hopeful journeys. There was very little in which to invest at home at the time. Others took their decisions to leave after partition with India in 1947 because of the tensions in the mountainous border regions of Azad Kashmir.

They were welcomed into West Yorkshire and cities like Bradford because their labour was needed. They were willing to work unpopular shifts in the mills and keep the machines running twenty-four hours a day. They were ready to do the jobs that other workers did not want to do and they often accepted lower wages and worse working conditions. As a group, these men contributed a great deal to the economy of the region in the post-war period. Their labour meant that the textile mills remained productive for several years longer than they would otherwise have done. They did not plan to stay, intending rather to earn money as quickly as possible and then return home to build houses for their families. When the mills started closing down and the wages drying up in the 1970s, they might have returned to their families in South Asia or perhaps sought more lucrative employment in the burgeoning economies of the Middle East. But this did not happen for reasons we will see later.

At the start, the community was overwhelmingly male. But women's rôles were to become important later, as the next chapter will show. The men usually arrived in Bradford alone, leaving wives and children at home. They were invariably very poor. Because of this, the domestic lives they constructed were quite different from those of their neighbours. They formed tightly knit, self-sufficient communities. This no doubt afforded them security and solidarity, but their lives were hard. Singh (1994) points out how their concentration in the inner city led to a 'vicious cycle of general deprivation'. This had, and is still having, effects on the development of the city as a whole. From the start, they hardly mixed with other people. They lived as cheaply as possible in groups, usually of relatives from the same villages and towns in Pakistan. They quickly established their own communal support networks for cooking and other domestic needs. Some of the canteens and cafés established in the 1950s and 1960s developed into restaurants which still flourish today. The new arrivals were generally not interested in the social or cultural events going on around them in the city, most of which must have seemed strange to young Muslim men from faraway countries. So the young men spent most of their early years in Bradford hardly ever seeing and almost certainly never speaking to people from different backgrounds to their own. Consequently, many of them never learned to speak English. In turn, the people living around them never really got to know them.

The housing arrangements of the new arrivals have also had a lasting influence on the make-up of the city. Singh (1994) suggests that the patterns of settlement 'did not support the development of a harmonious multicultural and multilingual society' in Bradford, resulting as they did in lack of opportunities for communication and mixing between groups of different backgrounds. The young men clubbed together to rent houses from private landlords in the inner city wards. These houses were often of poor quality and poorly maintained. Earlier waves of immigrants had been happy to leave them behind for better accommodation in the suburbs. But this did not happen for the men from Pakistan. They bought up many of these houses by supporting each other in self-help loan schemes. They doubtless had aspirations to move on, but were often prevented from moving from the inner city to more attractive areas of the district. The discriminatory practices of estate agents and building societies, who systematically denied them access to property in more agreeable suburban areas and to mortgages to buy them, made sure of this. This has led to many of the families remaining in the same inner city wards to this day. It has contributed to the segregation of the city and thus to some of its current problems.

For most of these adventurous young men, the desire to return in success to the homeland was never fulfilled. They did go on regular visits to maintain contact with – and add to – their families and to oversee the building projects initiated with their remittances. Then in 1962 the British Government introduced an Immigration Act which had immediate and dramatic effects. The legislation was hastily introduced in Britain in a climate of fear and apprehension and it was to have tremendous long-term consequences for both Britain and Pakistan, though not those for which the government hoped. Fearful of permanent separation from their wives and children, many of the men decided not to continue with their regular visits home but to bring their families to Britain instead. Consequently one result of the Immigration Act was that a large number of wives and children came to join their husbands and fathers in Britain in the late 1960s and early 1970s. Paradoxically, a law which was intended to curtail immigration into Britain had the effect of increasing it for a time.

At the same time, the long economic boom in Bradford was slowly coming to an end. As the mills began to close down, there was nothing much to replace them. The South Asian men had to compete with the poorly qualified section of the white population for the few jobs available outside the mills. It was just the wrong time for the sudden and rapid growth of the community and for the arrival of so many dependants too. Because so many women and children came in, calls on the social services increased hugely. The number of Commonwealth (including Pakistan) immigrant children in schools in Bradford increased from 962 to 4,686 between 1963 and 1968. Moreover, because of the pattern of settlement, the children were all concentrated in a small number of schools in three inner city wards. Halstead (1988) reports that by 1965, twelve Bradford schools had 25% immigrant children on roll, and by 1984 there were nineteen schools, all in three inner city wards, with over 70% of children on roll from ethnic minorities.

This sudden and highly visible evidence of a large and growing ethnic minority community must have caused alarm in the minds of longer-established Bradfordians. Horace Hird, who was a member of Bradford Council from 1944-1968 and Mayor from 1951-52, expresses some of the feeling of the time in his locally published *Bradford in History*:

> ... let us remember that neither Bradford nor Keighley nor any other place will have happy citizens if they become hopelessly choked with people whose way of life and habits are so much at variance from our own ...

His words echo those of contemporary national politicians, who were busily spreading anxiety in many parts of the country among the 'ethnic majority' population about the threat posed by immigrants to their livelihoods and ways of life. Even though successive waves of arrivals had over many years been assimilated into Bradford and had contributed to its richness in many ways, the signs did not look good for the groups from South Asia. It seemed as if they would not easily be integrated into the city.

So by the 1980s there were large, well-established South Asian communities living in Bradford. Many families, now reunited, lived in close proximity with relatives from home in the same streets that the men had settled in years before. Their children were growing up, marrying into extended family networks in the traditional ways and beginning to have children of their own. This all added to the richness of the communities, to their stability and happiness, and to their opportunities for mutual support in times of distress. It also meant that traditional values and attitudes were strongly maintained, often to a greater extent than in Pakistan itself. I went to Pakistan in 1993 with a group of education students, many of them of Pakistani heritage. Some had never been 'home' before. They were surprised to find that certain things were done there in much more liberal ways than they were back in Bradford. They commented on how their lives in England seemed to be 'behind the times' compared to some of the customs they saw in Pakistan.

There is no doubt that the closeness and conformity of the South Asian communities in Bradford have had negative effects on their relationships with other groups in the city and on their own development. First, their separateness from other communities has inhibited everyday cross-cultural communication and has done nothing to encourage mutual friendships and understanding. Instead, suspicion prevails on both sides. At times of tension, this has flared up into anger and violence. Second, the young people, as they are gaining western education and economic freedom, have begun to see for themselves that there are other ways of doing things. Many of them want to try these enticing new ways for themselves. More aware than their parents of the problems and contradictions of modern urban life, they sometimes feel the need to make choices and compromises that they can't share with their parents. Education has had a central rôle to play in these – often painful – changes.

Education and response to diversity

As in other industrial cities in Britain, education became a huge concern in Bradford in the mid-nineteenth century. The awareness of the need to improve the lot of the factory workers was reflected in the twin Victorian ideals of Christian philanthropism and commercialism. W. E. Forster, a key national figure in the debates, was MP for Bradford from

1861 to 1886. He owned a textile mill in the city. He was the architect of the 1870 Act which introduced compulsory elementary education. Forster received great acclaim in London for this, but Bradfordians were not so sure about the benefits of educational reform. As the Act was being praised to the skies in London, Forster's constituents were meeting in St. George's Hall in Bradford. They passed their usual vote of thanks to their MP, but added an amendment expressing their disapproval of the Act. Forster's response was perceptive and straightforward, 'You have only done what I have always expected Bradford people to do – to say what you think.'

After such a robust start, the development of education in Bradford was bound to be interesting. The first Bradford School Board was established in September 1870. Its members appeared to represent commercial rather than academic interests. Ten out of the sixteen were businessmen or artisans. They set about the task of building the first Board Schools and eight were completed by 1874. Five of them are still in use in the inner city today. They were impressive buildings, built out of Yorkshire stone in an 'ornate ecclesiastical Gothic style of architecture', much more extravagant and expensive than those being built in other parts of the country. They attracted much admiration – the angels in the roof beams of Lilycroft School were particularly praised – but inevitably, also, criticism for their lavishness. They symbolised the seriousness with which the board members viewed their task of developing education in Bradford. It has been suggested that:

> ... set amongst mills and row upon row of back-to-back houses, these buildings served to illustrate and to emphasise a genuine pride in the job in hand, demonstrating that the task of educating all children was a task of importance, of distinction. (City of Bradford Corporation, 1970)

The opulence of Gothic architecture and Yorkshire stone has been long lasting, but the intake into the schools today is quite unlike that in the 1870s. Because they are virtually all located in inner city wards, most of the children being educated in the old Board Schools today are from the Pakistani heritage communities I have just described. These are the schools which housed those children who came to join their fathers in Bradford in the 1960s. Their children, and now sometimes their grandchildren, are following them into the classrooms.

As the intake into the schools changed, the South Asian communities were quick to mobilise in order to express their concerns about some aspects of their children's schooling. The Bradford Muslim Parents' Association was formed in 1974. Bradford Council realised the need to make adjustments. At first, they reacted to concerns raised by the parents about daily practices in schools rather than setting any kind of agenda themselves. Specific issues which they dealt with were single sex schooling and the observance of Islamic practices in terms of assemblies, uniforms, swimming and school dinners. Members of other communities began to complain that the needs of Muslim children were being placed ahead of their own. White parents began to seek places for their children in schools out of the inner city, so exacerbating the segregation. The situation was complex. There needed to be calm and reasoned discussion about all these sudden changes. This could have informed and modified attitudes among all those involved in the processes of education and might have led to collaborative development of principled policy to guide daily practice in the longer term. This never seemed to happen.

Teachers working in the inner city schools were at the sharp end of dealing with the changes and experiencing diversity on a day-to-day basis. As in the country as a whole, the numbers of ethnic minority teachers in Bradford schools has always been low. Most teachers knew very little about the South Asian children, the languages they spoke, their cultures and religions. Little information was available at the time to provide them with background knowledge and there was certainly nothing in their training or professional development in this. Teachers and pupils inhabited different social and cultural worlds and there were few bridges between them. David Shepherd was a teacher in Bradford in the 1980s. He saw, even then, that this cultural and linguistic divide between teachers and their pupils was one of the main underlying causes of the underachievement of the children. His ethnographic study (Shepherd, 1987) of 28 teachers in one middle school led him to the conclusion that it was the lack of any co-constructed discourses which blocked so harmfully the communication between teachers and learners. Teachers simply had no shared language with which to talk to their pupils, and no shared culture to talk about.

In his article, Shepherd quotes extensively from the interviews he conducted with the teachers and their negative views about the children come through strongly. They rarely refer to their pupils by name but instead speak in terms of a largely undifferentiated mass, often labelled 'these children'. The following are typical comments:

... very few of the parents are interested in education at all ...

... the girls don't show as much interest in academic work ...

... I have a class and I'm teaching them, and I know sixty per cent won't know what I'm talking about ...

... with things as they stand now there's no solution. You're banging your head against a brick wall all the time ...

I remember hearing almost identical comments when I was teaching in an inner city school in Bradford in the 1980s. At the time I found them confusing as they did not match my perceptions of the children or parents that I met. What was more troubling for me was that they were made by sincere and dedicated teachers who worked hard to help their pupils, and worried when they did not seem to succeed. But the attitudes they reflected contributed to – and were also partly a result of – the low expectations that was part of the culture of failure that existed at the time and still exists today.

Attacks on diversity

While contradictions such as those just described worked away on teachers' and pupils' morale like a relentlessly dripping tap, controversy of a more ferocious nature was about to erupt. In July 1982, Ray Honeyford, headteacher of an inner city middle school, wrote a letter to the local newspaper in which he criticised council policy on education. This was the start of a sorry saga that was to last more than three years. During that time, Honeyford was invited to Downing Street by Margaret Thatcher and was the subject of an adjournment debate in the House of Commons. In its painful course, the 'Honeyford affair' also attracted international attention – I remember hearing of it in 1985 while I was living in Sierra Leone. Halstead (1988) provides a full account and chronology of the affair. The events involved were not particularly physically violent compared with happenings in other cities in Britain at the time but rather a battle of words and ideas, and so in some ways more dangerous. There is no doubt that they have done enduring damage to the development of a dialogue about education among the different communities in the city.

Before his appointment in Bradford in 1980, Honeyford had worked as an English teacher and part-time University tutor for many years in the Manchester area. He had published articles on education espousing views which were in tune with the New Right ideologies which were to underpin the Conservative government's radical educational reforms in the 1980s. His main target for attack became Bradford Council. Like many teachers with similar working-class origins, strong personal commitment and powerful ambition, he resented what he considered to be undue interference in his professional autonomy by LEA advisers and bureaucrats. At the time, Bradford Council were working on their twelve-point plan *Turning Point* which proposed a new approach to race relations. Honeyford believed that such reforms undermined the values he thought the council should be upholding. He was particularly incensed about the Racism Awareness Training courses which all headteachers were expected to attend. In his writing, Honeyford makes constant reference to the need for education to promote the best of 'British' cultural values, articulated in terms such as the following:

> ... this country is a unique nation with great achievements in learning, the arts, science, literature, the military arts and diplomacy ... we have played a leading rôle in the establishment of parliamentary democracy and the rule of law ... the English are a people of a distinctive character ... the need ... to respect, cherish and be properly proud of one's national origin and identity ... (Honeyford, 1986)

This is the model of culture which, as we saw in Chapter One, underpinned the formation of the National Curriculum in the 1980s and 1990s. It reflects a popular and seductive view of what it means to be English. But it is a model which constructs culture as fixed, static and resistant to change. It does not recognise the fluid, constantly changing nature of society and the ways in which notions of Englishness are changing too. With this static view of culture goes the belief that it is the rôle of the school to help safeguard and nurture its products and to promote a sense of national identity in order to maintain social cohesion.

Honeyford appeared to be sincere in his opinions, but politicians cynically hijacked his ideas for their own ends. In April 1985, Marcus Fox, Conservative MP for Shipley, a constituency adjoining Bradford, started an adjournment debate in the House of Commons, claiming that Honeyford had been denied freedom of speech. This was a ludicrous notion considering that Honeyford's articles had already been reprinted from small journals into wide circulation newspapers such as *The Times* and he had also been invited to write for the *Daily Mail*. Meanwhile, the voices of his opponents were hardly heard in the mainstream media. Fox was, in effect, denying them the very freedom of speech he was claiming to be so important for all. A quotation from the opening of the parliamentary speech (taken from van Dijk, 1993) illustrates the ways in which the politician delegitimises their viewpoints and thus silences their voices:

> This matter has become a national issue – not from Mr. Honeyford's choice. Its consequences go beyond the issue of race relations or, indeed, of education. They strike at the very root of our democracy and what we cherish in this House above all – the freedom of speech. One man writing an article in a small-circulation publication has brought down a holocaust on his head. To my mind, this was a breath of fresh air in the polluted area of race relations ...

We could say much about this dangerous language and its harmful effects on any ongoing debate about multiculturalism. Such connotatively loaded words as 'holocaust' and 'polluted' should not be used lightly. Fox could only make his assertions with impunity because of his position and the setting in which he made them. They are breathtaking in their inaccuracy and negative stereotyping. Yet, they are fairly typical of the right wing political discourse on multiculturalism of the time, reported freely in the mass media.

Further on in the speech, Fox calls Honeyford's opponents 'Marxists' and 'Trots', and suggests that they do not belong to 'the silent majority of decent people'. He thus implies that they are somehow to be excluded from 'normal' society. Sentiments like this, voiced in different contexts, add fuel to the inflammatory arguments of such groups as the National Front. They do injustice to the members of society who most need the opportunity to have their voices heard, their contributions validated and their interests protected. As Foster-Carter (1987) reminds us, freedom of speech 'demands respecting the rights and freedom of others and not inciting hatred between fellow human beings'. Fox's speech represents a cynical and irresponsible attempt to take advantage of a complex, confused and emotionally charged situation for his personal and political ends.

Besides the freedom of speech issue, a principal contradiction of the affair is the way the term 'racist' was used. Though accused of racism, Honeyford constantly denied the charge, which, as Halstead records, he described as 'a failure of the human spirit and odious'. While this is a typical response to the charge of racism in 'élite discourse' (van Dijk, 1999), there is evidence that Honeyford did have strong commitment to the children in his school and genuine respect for some aspects of South Asian culture. I have met former pupils who say they genuinely liked him. No doubt he was appalled, confused and hurt by the force of the reaction to him. Such confusions are part of the whole debate about multiculturalism, but we need to analyse them, not gloss them over. Perhaps the saddest effect of the affair is the way it contributed to a closing down of discussion and dialogue about multicultural and anti-racist issues in Bradford. Foster-Carter (1987) suggests that it had a national effect on moves to enhance equality of opportunity. Other LEAs became reluctant to take on unions and other groups after seeing the problems faced by Bradford LEA. Discussions about diversity became much more difficult towards the end of the 1980s, at a time when they should have been central to debates about education and the embryonic National Curriculum. This was failure on a national level. It has contributed much to the continuing underachievement of children whose distinctive knowledge and experiences need to be made central to their education in order for them to succeed.

This, then, was the context from which my own questions grew about why some children could succeed in school, apparently against the odds, in a system which seemed to offer them so little opportunity to do so.

Researching diversity
When I began to work in primary teacher training, I had the opportunity to visit classrooms in different schools, sometimes in different countries. I was able to observe and compare the wide range of ways pupils and teachers had of talking and working together. I described in

Chapter One the theories that began to form in my mind about the rôles of language and culture in successful teaching and learning. I wanted to find out more about what helped some children to succeed. Perhaps this could answer some of my own questions, and even be useful to other teachers. I decided to carry out a small-scale study of a group of 'successful' learners as they progressed through Key Stage Two in Bradford schools (which were, at the time I started, still operating under a three-tier system). I wanted to work in a fairly typical school, but one with a mixed intake, if possible, in order to explore the possible influences of different languages and cultures on children's learning.

In the end, I was welcomed by the headteacher into a school that I did not know very well. The children who went there came from families originating in Eastern Europe and Ireland as well as South Asia. It was in a residential area just out of the inner city with mixed, mostly private, housing. It was a fairly small first school with a nursery unit, catering for children from 3-9 years. The staff worked hard to develop a friendly atmosphere. They encouraged parents into the school to take part in jumble sales and social events as well as to consult their children's teachers. There was a bilingual Home School Liaison Officer. The school had a small catchment area and was very much part of a local community. Some parents had themselves been pupils there. Some of the staff lived locally and sent, or had sent, their own children there. The majority of the children progressed at the age of nine to the nearby middle school.

I was a visitor to the school for almost two years. By what turned out to be a happy chance, I was able to work in a vertically grouped class which had two class teachers working in a jobshare. This meant that I had the advantage of two skilled professionals to observe and discuss things with, and that we could all get to know each other. It also meant I could stay in the class with a group of children as they moved from Year Three to Year Four. About half the children in the class were mono-lingual English speakers. The bilingual children were predominantly Mirpuri Punjabi and/or Urdu speakers, with a small number having Pushto or Gujerati as their first language. As in most multilingual class-rooms in Britain, the children hardly used any other language but English in the classroom. I also observed very little use of different languages in the playground or other parts of the school. One could say that for most of the bilingual children in this school, English, rather than their mother tongue, was their first language.

I sometimes sat and observed in the classroom and the children saw me taking notes. They looked over my shoulder and tried to read what I was writing. Sometimes, they wrote their own comments alongside my notes. After I had been going into the class for a while and when the teachers felt comfortable, I began to use a tape recorder to have a better record of what was said. Occasionally, I took something related to the ongoing work of the class in to show the children, and the teachers asked me to talk to the whole class. At other times I worked with individuals or groups of children as directed by the teachers. In this situation, the tape recorder was usually running and I might also take notes of what was happening, usually saying to the children something like, 'that's interesting, I'm going to write it down.'

When the children moved into Year Five, I followed them into the middle schools they transferred to. Most of them went to the same school which was near the first school and one or two went to other schools in the area. One boy eventually moved on to a private school, and I was able to visit him there one day towards the end of his time in Year Five. Because the organisation in the middle schools was unlike that of the first school, I was unable to form a relationship with one class and its teachers. Instead, I visited periodically for the whole day and followed the children through their lessons, which were taken by several different teachers. I did this as often as I could until the children reached the end of Year Six when they were all officially deemed successful as they all attained at least Level Four in the SATs tests as they moved on to Key Stage Three.

As well as observing and talking to the children, I interviewed their teachers. In the first school, I got to know the two teachers very well and we had many discussions, but in the middle schools I could not talk to the teachers as much. I could not interview all the teachers who taught the children, but was able to talk at length with a group who volunteered and who were generous with their time and open and honest about their views. I realised the significance of these views for the ways they interacted with the children, so have included an account of them in Chapter Five.

SUMMARY OF KEY ISSUES

In this chapter, I have provided some historical background to the situation in Bradford. This gives a context for the material in the next three chapters about the children at home and at school, and about their teachers. These are some of the key points:

- Bradford's population is highly diverse because of its long history in textile manufacturing and trade

- The South Asian communities in Bradford, while adding to the richness and diversity of the city, have had distinctive problems in integrating with the other communities. The causes are largely historical, due to their patterns of settlement

- The history of education in Bradford is rich in controversy and contradiction, and this has made open and free debate about diversity and multiculturalism difficult to achieve

- Children's achievements in school have suffered because of these issues.

3

THE CHILDREN LEARNING AT HOME: COMMUNITY AND FAMILY INFLUENCES

When I began to observe the children at school, my original intention was to collect samples of talk only from within the four walls of the classroom. I planned to analyse them to try to determine what factors enabled the children to succeed. After several visits to the classroom, I began to realise that it was not so easy, as some of the factors which helped the children to succeed came from outside the classroom. I began to focus on a small group of bilingual children in the class who struck me as articulate and confident. Their teachers agreed that they could be regarded as 'successful learners'. Although only eight years old at the time, they seemed to have the successful bilinguals' confidence and facility with language identified in research by, for example, Bialystok (1991) and Cummins (1996). They coped easily with most of the cognitive demands of the work in the class, had well developed reading skills and generally produced writing of a higher standard than most of the other children. They were very interested in me and what I was doing. They plied me with questions about my work, my job, my family and anything else they wanted to know. Above all, these children were bright and confident; they seemed to have a clear sense of who they were and where they belonged. I began to realise that their home and family lives were very important to them and was fascinated by the bits of information they offered about these aspects of their experience.

As well as observing and working with the children in class, I began to chat with them at lunch time. I wanted to get to know them and to gain some idea of the ways they used English and possibly other languages in different contexts. There were five children – Nahida, Yasmin, Rehana, Anwar and Faisal (who later left the class). All were of Pakistani Muslim heritage and spoke either Urdu or Mirpuri Punjabi as their first language. On my weekly visits to their class, we would stay behind in the classroom at lunch time, eating our sandwiches and talking about all kinds of things. The class teachers often appeared towards the end of the lunch hour and joined in briefly. They were always interested in what was going on and positive in their responses to what the children said. This chapter begins by discussing some extracts from these informal conversations in order to illustrate something of the range of the children's out-of-school experiences and explain how I think they relate to their learning. After this, we hear from their families, mostly their mothers.

Informal talk at school

The lunch time audiotapes show the children using a much wider range of English in terms of grammatical structure, lexis and so on than they do in the tapes I made of the classroom conversations. The children speak only in English. The tapes indicate the children's range and wealth of experience acquired in totally different ways than their school learning. Here are three short extracts.

Extract One – Rehana's experiences in Pakistan

When we first began these conversations, Rehana had recently returned from a visit to Pakistan with her family. She enthusiastically told us stories about her experiences. She brought artifacts into school that the family had brought back with them. Rehana's visit to Pakistan meant that she missed about four weeks of school at the beginning of Year Four. Extended visits to Pakistan or elsewhere are often seen as a cause for concern because children miss out on their schooling. But such visits can also have positive outcomes. On Rehana's return, she was eager to join the lunch time group again and said she had lots to tell us about her visit. I asked the others to think of stories from Pakistan to tell also, as all except Yasmin had been there. The next week, Rehana greeted me on my arrival in the classroom with a list her father had written of the names of the places the family had travelled to in

Pakistan. We found as many of these as we could on a map. At lunch time, we settled to our conversation and Rehana began to tell us about a visit her family had made to some hot springs to carry out a medical treatment for one of the children. The springs were 'loads of far' from the house they were staying in:

01 Rehana   there was this river where it was so hot water and .. er .. my niece .. she had eczema and we took her there and we .. we put that hot water on her, and she got better .. and it was so hot that you couldn't touch it

05 JC: the water in the river was so hot?

Rehana: mm .. yeah

JC: so how did they put the water on your niece then if the water was so hot you couldn't touch it?

Rehana: well, this .. sort of ..

10 Nahida: well?

Rehana: no .. this sort of ... mm .. little place where the hot water didn't go on there .. mm .. there was cold water, so they put the cold water in a jug and then they got a cup and put some hot water, and put some cold water
15   .. then they put it on her

JC: then you poured it on her, did you?

Rehana: .. mm .. then my niece, she wanted to eat, and her mum brought an egg, and my mum put it .. er ... on .. er .. a stone, and she put .. um .. er ..

20 JC: the egg?

Rehana: no, she put this sort of .. er .. leaf sort of thing .. er

JC: mmm .. on the stone ..

Rehana: and then, she put the egg, and when my.. when my brother was going to get it, it was so hot he couldn't
25   touch it, and it was .. it was cooked!

Rehana's story arises from a meaningful and memorable personal experience that clearly affected her greatly. She shows considerable skill in storytelling and an intuitive understanding of how to structure a narrative. She has a strong purpose for her telling and captures the attention of her audience. She selects appropriate events to make the incident meaningful and interesting to her listeners. She provides an appropriate amount of detail, using more complex syntactic structures than she would normally use in her spontaneous talk. She handles questions from her listeners with skill, weaving them into the thread while maintaining the line of her story. Shrubshall (1997), in agreement with many others, argues for the importance of oral storytelling in children's early learning experiences and as a preparation for literacy. Rehana's oral text provides strong evidence for her potential for achievement in literacy.

In the way she tells her story, Rehana also demonstrates that she knows where she belongs, as a member of a closely-knit family and cultural group. Her use of pronouns to position herself within the narrative is interesting. In line 02, she is part of the 'we', the family group who took the sick child to the hot springs, whereas in lines 13-15, she talks about how 'they' poured the water on the child. At this point, Rehana has become the observer and teller of the story, aware that her audience may need more detailed information than she has so far given. She thus constructs her own social worlds, first as a member of a family group on an expedition to the hot springs, then as an individual with an interesting story to tell to an attentive audience.

Extract Two – Yasmin's account of a wedding

This extract is taken from a conversation early in Year Four where the children were telling stories about their families. The topic of weddings came up. Rehana greeted Yasmin's announcement that she was going to talk about her mother's wedding with incredulity, 'oh .. how did you born?' but Yasmin quickly solves the mystery of how she knows about an event that happened before she was born:

01	Yasmin:	my mum had a wedding before my .. before I was born because they made a film and I watched it
	JC:	oh .. right

05	Yasmin:	I've seen the film of it, and miss, you know, do you know what miss, my .. my dad wanted to sit down and my aunty never let him .. she wouldn't let him sit down, right, so she said, 'give me some money and then I'll get up,' and
10		my dad gave her some money and then she got up .. and then my dad sat separate, and my mum sat separate .. then someone sat in the middle of my mum and dad, and then, they said, 'you get up, let my mum and dad sit
15		together,' miss, it was at .. em .. 10 Jones Street
	JC:	oh .. in Bradford?
	Yasmin:	yeah, miss
	Nahida:	my uncle had wedding at Riverside, miss
	JC:	(to Yasmin) and what else happened?
20	Yasmin:	we went to a hall, miss, and ..
	Rehana:	we know that .. you always have a wedding in a hall
	JC:	(to Yasmin) yes, but you weren't ...
	Yasmin:	(to Rehana) no, sometimes they have it in a
25		home
	JC:	but you weren't there yet, were you
	Yasmin:	no miss, because .. because I've seen the film of it

Here again is a confident storyteller. Yasmin is just as actively engaged with her listeners as Rehana was. Like Rehana, she demonstrates her sense of belonging in the family and cultural network. The 'we' in line 20 and the references to 'my mum and dad' (lines 06-14) show that she regards herself as part of events that happened before she was born. In turn, the other children show by their comments that they share a clear understanding of how Asian weddings should be. There is no need for lengthy descriptions and details in Yasmin's story. Everyone knows what she is talking about. We can see in this how the children are developing as *cultural beings* through the process of *enculturation* (Cole, 1996).

They are becoming bicultural, actively learning how to be members of their own minority culture while operating effectively within the mainstream one.

Extract Three – Collaborative reading of an Urdu text

The third extract shows something of the positive cognitive effects of bilingualism, particularly in transferring reading strategies from one language to the other. On the day this was recorded, I had taken a dual language story book into school to read with the children. This motivated them to look for an Urdu book they knew was in the classroom. It turned out to be a rather formal reader with repetitive sentences about various animals, each illustrated with a small picture. The children began to read the book aloud together, arguing over and correcting each other's pronunciation of the Urdu words and discussing the best ways to translate them into English. In their reading of the Urdu, they provide examples of the kind of positive miscuing strategies revealed by miscue analysis (Arnold, 1982). They transfer skills which they have acquired in developing their fluency in reading English to the task of reading Urdu. Since they learn to read Urdu largely by rote, they would not be expected to apply such strategies to this task. In the extract, they are reading the sentence '*khargosh ghajar shawk se kah raha hai*' (the rabbit is eating the carrot happily):

01	3 ch. tog:	(spelling out) khargosh ... khargosh
	JC:	the rabbit ..
	Yasmin:	khargosh ..sh ..sh ..em.. gha .. gha
	Nahida:	ghu .. ghu ..
05	Yasmin:	khargosh .. gha ..
	Nahida:	heh .. spell it out .. gha ...
	Yasmin:	what's carrot in Urdu? ... ghajar
	Nahida:	ghajar ..
	Anwar:	ghajar ...
10	Yasmin:	ghajar ...
	Yasmin) Nahida):	ghajar .. sh .. shawk se kah raha hai ...

	Yasmin:	it means .. rabbit is eating ..
	Nahida:	the rabbit is eating happily the carrot
	JC:	the rabbit is happily eating the carrot
15	Yasmin) Nahida):	eating the carrot
	Yasmin:	yeah .. miss

The illustration in the book allows me to provide a cue for prediction (line 02), but the children ignore this and continue trying to decode the word '*ghajar*'. Nahida suggests a strategy, but is unable to get past the first syllable. Yasmin solves the problem by using the picture and translating the word from English into Urdu. At lines 08-10, the children are all pointing to the book and looking closely at the word '*ghajar*'. They then complete a correct reading of the sentence. Nahida's word order (line 13) does not correspond to the normal Urdu order (which would be *rabbit carrot happily eating is*). It is almost a hybrid of English and Urdu word order, with the adverb positioned in a possible, though not usual, place in relation to the verb in English and the noun at the end of the sentence, which can happen in either language. It is as if the two languages have become syncretised into a new and different whole here for the children. It is certainly a clear example of active processing of a reading text using all the language resources the children have at their disposal. It is also evidence for the ways literacy in one language can support literacy in another.

We can learn a great deal from these short extracts from the much longer informal conversations I held with this small group of multilingual children. They show the children's strong sense of belonging and confidence in their own cultures, and also their confidence in English. They show in different ways how what is regarded as success in an education system which claims to be *inclusive* can actually *exclude* the achievements of many of its participants. The implications of this are discussed fully in Chapters Six and Seven, but I would like to make a few points here, suggesting three factors necessary for *succeeding in diversity*, which I think the extracts demonstrate. These are:

- recognising the centrality of talk in supporting children's thinking and learning

- recognising the positive cognitive effects of bilingualism in different modes of language use

- understanding the importance of the rôle of culture in providing genuine equality of opportunity for all children

The extracts show the children to be expert and entertaining talkers. More than this, they are good listeners. They listen to each other and engage with each other's ideas. But in many primary classrooms, the chances children have to engage fully in collaborative, exploratory talk are severely limited. Opportunities to develop and display oral skills are becoming increasingly rare in mainstream classrooms generally, mainly because they do not figure in what officially counts for success. The pressure teachers feel to meet targets can lead them to provide pre-packaged, uniform teaching that takes no account of their pupils' own experiences. They believe they do not have time to listen to what the children themselves bring to their learning. The negative effects of this on the quality of learning in all classrooms, but especially in ethnically diverse classrooms, are worrying. What is needed is genuine support for teachers to build into their teaching opportunities for collaborative talk, the time and space to develop dialogues with their learners instead of having to resort to one-way transmission.

The second factor has been argued over for many years. Countless research projects have conclusively shown the positive cognitive benefits of bilingualism. But such benefits are still not exploited in most mainstream classrooms in England, chiefly perhaps because they are long term rather than short term. They take time to show themselves – the results in improved achievement in school are not immediately apparent. In their urgency to achieve the numerous NLS objectives, most teachers of multilingual children cannot find a way to value (or sometimes even acknowledge that they know about) their pupils' literacy skills and experience in languages other than English. Skutnabb-Kangas's waterlilies (1981) are still being sliced from their stems underwater; multilingual children's language and learning capacities are destroyed at the roots. Those teachers who do understand the cognitive implications of bilingualism find the opportunities for supporting bilingual learning in their classrooms severely limited by the need to produce quick results. The temptation is to provide a diluted and impoverished diet of worksheets and practice in answering test questions rather than opportunities for real cognitive and conceptual development.

Yet, as Wrigley (2000) attests when describing examples of successful ethnically diverse schools, it is possible to achieve the required results while recognising the need to support bilingual development. The ways to do this are too complex to be summed up in a quick set of bullet points. They involve dialogue rather than directives, empowerment rather than control for both teachers and learners. These issues are discussed in detail in Chapter Six.

The third factor – acknowledging the rôle of culture in learning – is perhaps less widely recognised than the other two. The ability to mediate different experiences displayed by the children in the extracts quoted above shows their self-confidence in negotiating the diverse worlds they live in. They provide evidence of what Knight (1994) calls *'pragmatic biculturalism'*. Knight reminds us that *culture* is more than *food and festivals*. She argues that children experience culture at two broad levels. There is the private culture of the home, which encompasses morality and a range of ways of behaving socially as well as practices related to dress, food and so on. And there is the public culture of school and other state and economic contexts. This is true for all children. But for children from most ethnic minority groups (and, Knight argues, working-class children) the gap between the two can be much wider than for children whose home backgrounds are closer to their teachers'. The inequities of power represented by such children's public and private worlds are much greater. Consequently, the potentially adverse effects on their success within the system are more severe.

The answer, surely, is not to pretend that such inequalities do not exist by treating all children as if they are the same. Knight sees as crucial the need to support and foster the development of what she calls *'bicultural acquisition'* in order to *'enable pupils to function with greater skill and understanding within the mainstream culture which controls their lives'* and so promote genuine equality of opportunity in inner city schools. Part of the way to achieve this is undoubtedly the valorising of the kinds of knowledge and skills which children bring to the classroom.

Family contexts

All the parents of the children in the study are of Pakistani heritage. Most of them were born in Pakistan to mothers who stayed behind while the fathers were working in Britain and making regular visits to the homeland. They are the sons and daughters of the men who formed the first distinct South Asian heritage community in Bradford, described in Chapter Two. They were brought to Britain at a very young age with their mothers as part of the wave of immigration of families into Bradford in the 1960s, so were the first generation of children to grow up in this specific British Asian context. The exception, Rehana's mother, lived for a few years as a young bride and mother in Pakistan and came to England with her two oldest children (now in their twenties) as infants in about 1980. All the parents, apart from Rehana's mother, speak English to high degrees of fluency. Some of them attended the same first and middle schools as their children – the focus of the study – subsequently did. They provide positive rôle models for their children of success in the British education system. This is especially true of Anwar's family. Anwar's mother, Parveen, was about three years old when she arrived from Pakistan with her mother and five siblings in the mid-1960s. She remembers their father meeting them at Manchester Airport with a transit van and driving them all to Bradford. She is now a qualified primary teacher. All her siblings (there were ultimately seven) have achieved similar success as lawyers, doctors, accountants and teachers.

All the families have strong links with relatives in Pakistan, maintained by extended visits 'home' of the whole family, or by short visits to England of relatives. Rehana's father has built a large house in his natal district of Mirpur. The whole family spent two years there when Rehana was a small child. In Bradford, all the children live in extended family households, with close relatives nearby, if not in the same house. All the families keep in close touch with relatives, some of them living nearby and others in other cities in England or Scotland. The children's playmates tend to be siblings and cousins rather than neighbours.

The first home visit I made was to Yasmin's house. I went one afternoon after school with Yasmin and her little sister, Arifa. I had not expected to make the visit on that day, as I had just given the children letters to take home to their parents the week before. But both girls were clearly expecting it, so off we went. My field notes, dictated to myself onto a tape recorder directly afterwards, give an impression of the nature and quality of this visit:

> Yasmin's little sister, Arifa, appeared at the classroom door and said, 'Are you coming to our house?' We set off, deciding it was better to go in the car than to walk. On the way, Arifa said something about Yasmin not being happy about boys in school and Yasmin kept wondering aloud whether we should go to the front door or the back door. We arrived at the back door and Y. was still undecided if this was the right thing to do. We went inside to an immaculate and huge kitchen with elaborate fireplace, two settees and a beautiful rug filling most of the floor space, baby asleep on one settee and grandmother (?) watching over her.
>
> Y. was very unsure of what to do, but conscious of the need for etiquette – she invited me up to her bedroom. She and Arifa put scarves over their heads then went off to find their mother. I was left with grandma and sleeping baby. We smiled at each other, then more people arrived – a silent boy (who turned out to be a cousin in Yr. 7 at Windyhill), two women (one young, one old) and a small child. Y. and A. came back, got changed and the youngest woman made a cup of tea. The children sat in the corner of the room, Y. smiling proudly at me. Eventually, Mum arrived with two little girls, followed soon by Dad and another man. Mum polite, articulate; Dad rather wary and taciturn. So there we were, sitting on the two settees; two grandmothers (who were sisters), mother, father, aunt, uncle and six children, including the baby, who woke up, totally calm, to be absorbed into the group.
>
> Y's mother engaged me in conversation about what I was doing – she had clearly read the letter carefully (sent previously to ask permission to visit) and was interested to know what I thought about her daughter's ability and progress. Her father had a few, incisive questions, 'How will it help Yasmin?' and whether any other children were involved. When I told him there were four, he asked if they were all Asian. He asked me about other schools I worked in, and worked out dates and places immediately when I told him. The problem about boys and Y. was discussed – she had been assigned a male 'guardian' for when she starts at Windyhill next term and was upset about it, because – as her mother explained – 'We like to

keep girls and boys separate'. The Yr. 7 cousin chipped in and explained that he was a guardian for another child, and that the school had reorganised things by giving some Yr. 7 girls two first school girls to 'guard' so that everyone had a same-sex guardian, but there were 'too much girls' this year. This was all gravely discussed and considered by the family group, the grandmothers smiling approval. Y's mother explained that they hadn't really had time to think about the letter I had sent because two uncles had died in Pakistan, brothers to the Grandmas, and one of the grandmothers wasn't well. They were still having a lot of visitors. She said they would be happy for me to come back and talk more, so that's where we left it. I left them all sitting there, a safe and comfortable extended family group – Y. beaming with satisfaction – I think she was pleased that things had gone so well.

Many of the impressions I gained from this first visit were deepened by further visits to Yasmin's house, and to the other families. I was made aware of warm, close communities where there is a great deal of mutual support, where the needs of individuals are absorbed into the group. Members of the family are expected to abide by unspoken rules which usually entail placing the needs of the group before those of the individual. Anwar's mother summed up the importance of family ties for her, 'The foundation is your family ... if that is weak, you're gone ...' . Against this background, everyone has an opportunity to express their views on matters of common concern. Yasmin's anxiety about being looked after by a boy in middle school – and the family's response – illustrates this. In this way the children were experiencing talk in their home contexts as a channel through which decisions are jointly made and as a medium for the collaborative construction of the culture of the family. I suggest that this could provide a model for the ways in which talk can be a medium for the negotiation of meaning. The children's home experiences of talk of this nature can influence the ways in which they participate in conversations in the classroom.

Attitudes towards heritage languages and cultural practices

In all the families, there was strong motivation to maintain heritage languages, culture and religion, alongside awareness of the need to achieve success in western terms. All the children could read and write Urdu.

They learnt it at community schools or at home. All were also learning the Koran in Arabic at various mosques. The methods by which they were being taught these languages often contrasted sharply with those employed in mainstream school. This makes the example of reading Urdu described above (p.46) all the more interesting and reinforces the case for transference from one language to another. There were only limited opportunities for the children to use languages other than English in school, and they rarely did so. There was no reason why they should. But when there was an awareness on the part of their school teachers of the languages they speak, read and write, and a recognition of the importance of home and community literacy practices as part of their whole experience of literacy, this seemed to have beneficial effects on the children's learning. The teachers in the first school seemed to recognise this. When I told them about the reading in Urdu, they expressed great interest, praised the children involved and invited the rest of the class to listen to the tape during the carpet time that afternoon. By the time the children reached middle school, however, such positive attitudes were no longer apparent and any overt reference to the children's home languages seemed to have disappeared.

The first school teachers seemed to perceive that a positive attitude to first language literacy would benefit literacy learning in English. For the parents on the other hand, the practices of reading and writing Urdu and reading the Koran were important more because they were seen to help reinforce acceptable standards of behaviour. The parents frequently expressed the view that it was essential for their children to be polite to and show respect for others. They believed that these qualities would be enhanced by an awareness of their cultural heritage and traditions. Anwar's mother, Parveen, described how, when she was a child, her father forbade her to speak English in the home. Her parents, newcomers to Britain in the 1960s and knowing virtually nothing about their new country, clearly felt the need to be strict with their children lest they be influenced by the negative social behaviour they observed around them. Her mother connected the maintenance of their home language with the maintenance of their culture. She resisted the pressure to move to English herself and never did. As Parveen expressed it, 'they thought the language was going to take away their culture'. This anxiety is still echoed by most of the parents of Parveen's generation but is expressed in different ways. In her comments about contemporary western television, Yasmin's mother, for example, was concerned about the 'foul language' transmitted in mainstream programmes. She would not allow her children to watch them.

At times the parents revealed complex attitudes to their heritage languages and to their own experiences of growing up in Bradford in the 1970s and 1980s. Parveen explained how she now felt she was at 'an advantage' because she was a fluent bilingual. She regretted the fact that her sons were not as fluent in Urdu as she would like them to be. Because her parents never learned to speak English, her children had to speak Urdu to their grandparents, which they could not do fluently. She considered her sons' mother tongue to be English because they 'think, speak and everything in English'. Her son, Anwar, concurred with this and said that he felt it would be 'a bit strange' to speak Urdu rather than English to his brothers. Despite her acceptance of the situation, Parveen regretted it and described how she felt knowledge of Urdu would make things easier for the children because, 'in effect, they have to fit into two cultures'. She recognised how she and her brothers and sisters had to do this as they were growing up thirty years earlier. Forbidden to speak English at home and denied the opportunity to use her first language in school, Parveen's own acquisition of English was not easy. She talks about being 'zipped up in school' because she 'did not dare speak' her first language, until eventually her competence in English overtook her Urdu.

Such honest and thoughtful comments as Parveen's need appropriately sensitive responses. They show the important and intimate connections between language and identity. They demonstrate the need for carefully considered approaches in policy and practice to language issues in education and the wider society. Parveen's ability to reflect upon the links between home and school and the importance of bilingualism to individual self-confidence clearly stem from personal experience and are no doubt enhanced by her experiences during teacher training and working as a bilingual teacher in ethnically diverse classrooms. This combination has led her to understand the importance of the kind of 'pragmatic biculturalism' for both teachers and children advocated by Knight (1994) and which the children display in their facility in moving between the diverse worlds of home and school. However, as a parent anxious to seek good schools for her children, Parveen faces the complexities and contradictions created by a system which does not value such facility, defines success in very narrow terms and then offers little consolation for those who fail according to the terms it imposes.

Anwar's grandparents and those of the other children who have lived as families in Bradford since the early 1960s have never learnt to speak English. As I suggested in the last chapter, their reluctance was perhaps due to their feeling very little sense of belonging to the society in which they found themselves. But the opportunities did not readily present themselves and the advantages were not immediately apparent. Anwar's grandfather worked in mills his whole working life on the shifts which no one else but fellow Pakistani immigrants were willing to work. His grandmother spent her time in the home taking care of a large family, with little of anything to spare. Their children all grew to be fluent and articulate English speakers, making their own way in a world which was alien to their parents. Now, when their British-born grandchildren are seen more as native English speakers than speakers of their heritage languages, it seems mistaken and unhelpful – or, at best, simplistic and misguided – to suggest that current problems in the community are a result simply of their reluctance to learn English.

Attitudes to education: contradictions and their consequences

All the parents had high aspirations for their children and were interested in what they were doing in school. They were keen to support them in carrying out school-related projects; they wanted to be involved. They recognised the crucial importance of gaining qualifications for future success through western education. They believed that success in school was achieved by hard work, rather than through individual ability. They saw educational attainment as leading to good careers, and the opportunity to 'be somebody'. This belief did not seem to be influenced by gender, though because they were talking to me, a white, female researcher, the mothers may have felt they should say what they thought I hoped to hear. But the fathers I spoke to shared such attitudes. Of all the parents, Nahida's mother demonstrated the strongest aspirations for her child. She clearly associated academic success with social status:

> I really like her to go in top group, so, you know, once you are in top group, you can meet nice people.. nice things around you, and she can be better off .. I'd like her to be somebody, you know ...

Similarly, Yasmin's mother, who has four daughters, could see the advantage for girls of gaining academic qualifications before marriage:

> You've got to fix it in their minds that they have to get their education. that's the most important thing in their life. Nobody can take that away from them, they've got to achieve something, then we can decide ...

Sentiments like these seem to contradict the commonly held view that the parents of Muslim girls do not encourage their daughters to pursue education but prefer them simply to prepare for marriage at an early age.

In line with the sense that individual opinions were subjugated to those of the group, the parents did not make decisions about their children's education on their own. Other members of the extended family had their say and everyone's view was taken into account. The same was true of other major decisions of family life. All the parents used the pronoun *'we'* continually in their narratives to describe joint decisions and regular family practices such as visits from relatives, watching television, preparing and eating meals. Before I got to know Yasmin's family, her aunt (who lived in the family household) had gained a place at a University in the south of England to study Law. But no-one was happy with this idea. Yasmin's mother described the way a transfer was arranged to a local university, so that the aunt could stay at home:

> ... she started crying because they wouldn't give her a place at University in A. and she didn't want to go out to B. because that was too far away, so we actually finally got her a place in A. which is quite near where we are, only 20 minutes away. We didn't want her so far away, we don't want to leave her on her own there ...

While their mother was telling me this, Yasmin and Arifa sat beside her on the settee, nodding and smiling. About a year later, when I was making another visit, I noticed on the sitting room wall a large framed photograph of the aunt in her graduation gown.

No one would seriously dispute the need for parents to take an active rôle in order for their children to succeed in school. Studies such as those by Pollard (1996) confirm this. Pollard's work in white, largely middle class social contexts shows the ease with which shared understandings between teachers and parents can be developed when they have much in common, and the beneficial effects of this on the children's learning. In contrast, Sharp and Green (1975), working in a mainly white working class context, found that the teachers in the school they studied had very negative views about the parents and their ability to support their children's education. They show how these attitudes had a detrimental effect on the children's learning. One of their conclusions was that parents needed to '*comply*' with teachers' views of what should happen in classrooms. Parents, suggest Sharp and Green, must be able to show that they understand and agree with the teachers' opinions and attitudes, in other words, to play the rôle of '*good parent*', but according to the teacher's definitions. Sharp and Green see this as very much connected to issues of power. If the teachers, who have '*more powerful purchase on the situation*' in the classroom, form negative judgements about the parents, this will adversely affect the expectations they have about the children's learning potential. It seems that if parents do not come up to teachers' expectations, it is hard for their children to do so.

The only parent in the study who reported any difficulties in communication between herself and school was Anwar's mother, Parveen. This was interesting, as she herself was a qualified teacher. She felt that there was no dialogue between herself and her son's teachers, something she said she 'yearned for'. She could find no opportunity for conversation with the teachers and felt ignored. In turn, the two teachers in the first school class, while very positive about their relationships with parents generally, confessed to finding her a little difficult to talk to. Perhaps part of the difficulty was that Parveen did not meet the teachers' expectations of a 'good' Asian parent. This is discussed more fully in the next section, where I consider just what is meant by 'a good education' here.

Apart from Anwar's, all the families felt that they enjoyed positive relationships with their children's teachers and schools. But issues surrounding parental choice worried them, especially as the children moved through middle school and decisions had to be made about the next steps. Seeing me perhaps as an authority figure, all the parents sought my advice and opinions about local schools and listened carefully to my comments, such as they were. For most of the families, decisions about which middle schools to send their children to seemed to be made on the grounds of proximity (because the children were regarded as too young to travel far from home) and familiarity. 'We know the people going there', Nahida's father told me. Parveen (Anwar's mother) was the only one who expressed her reasons for choice of middle school in terms of 'quality'. Anwar went on to a different middle school from the other three children in the study because his mother considered it better. His older brothers had also attended there, though they had since moved on to a private school.

A 'good education'

Parveen's quest was to secure a 'good education' for her three sons within the mainstream system. She articulated clearly and forcefully the frustrations, as she saw them, entailed in such a quest. These short extracts from two of the long conversations I had with her about these issues illustrate her concerns.

Conversation One – finding the right school

I asked Parveen why she had chosen this middle school for Anwar. This led her into relating Anwar's experiences of attending several different first schools, none of which seemed able to provide what his mother was looking for. Anwar began his schooling at a first school near his home, which had a high percentage of ethnic minority children on roll. Parveen quickly removed him from this school because she felt that his ability to read was not being recognised. He then began to attend a primary school, which I call 'Leafylane', with few ethnic minority children, along with his brothers and cousins. Different problems arose here. This is part of what Parveen said about the two schools:

01	Parveen:	I taught them reading at home, I went through
		the schemes etcetera, so by three or four, they
		were reading books. So when I got to school, I
		actually witnessed this, you know .. there was
05		.. there, my son was sitting there .. that's the
		reason why we took them to Leafylane, you
		see .. and the education was much better there,
		it were a higher standard because there was a
		lot of ... you know, white children rather than
10		Asians. I mean they were, I actually saw this,
		you know, when I was waiting outside in the
		cloakroom, they were saying, 'this is the door

.. this is the so ... ' ah, I was really hurt .. um ..
you know, he was just sitting there, bored. So
15   when I tried to tell them that he knows how to
read, I don't think they were interested, and
that really hurt as well, you know, and I
thought, well you're supposed to be
negotiating with the parents and the teachers
20   and I was not happy when they were just, and
they just sort of ignored me .. and I thought ..
well .. er .. I was really upset you know . You
feel as if you've put hard work into it, and
they're going to sort of maintain and carry it
25   forward. Well, obviously they've got to
differentiate, but he was just sitting there in
that class .. I felt so sorry for him, he was
sitting .. and I thought he was just wasting his
time ...

This extract starts with Parveen talking about her unhappiness about the way teachers at Anwar's first school discounted her pre-school efforts to teach him to read. She describes her feelings at seeing him sitting with the rest of the class repeating simple sentences in English after the teacher. The teachers appeared to be using a direct ESL-oriented approach to teaching the children English vocabulary and grammar that seems better suited to teaching adults. Aside from the probability that many of the children would have known more English than the level of input indicated here suggests, this approach is not really appropriate for young children. But Parveen's feelings about it seem to go beyond impersonal professional judgement. She uses strongly emotional words to describe her feelings: she talks about being 'really hurt' (lines 13 and 17); 'not happy'(line 20); 'really upset' (line 22) and feeling 'so sorry' for her son (line 27). She seems to feel personally attacked by the problems she perceives in the school provision. There is the same powerful sense of hurt in the way she talks about feeling 'ignored' by the teachers. They did not appear to be interested in discussing with her the kind of provision she thought her son needed. In a later conversation, she spoke of her 'yearning' for a dialogue with her children's teachers which was never fulfilled. While such feelings may not be exclusive to an ethnic minority parent such as Parveen, her undoubted cultural distance from the teachers made her feel that the gap between them was immense, possibly unbridgeable. She had much more to say on this issue, as we shall see.

This extract also reveals Parveen's implicit belief that 'good' schools are those with few 'Asian' children (lines 09-10). I asked her later about this, and she confirmed that this was indeed what she thought. Other parents in the study held the same view and this surprised me. On the face of it, it appears inconsistent with Parveen's beliefs about the importance of maintaining her heritage culture and language. She seems to be denying her and her children's identity when assessing the educational standards of the schools. From another viewpoint, however, it is a sensible response to the situation. If the evidence from performance league tables is taken as an indication of the quality of the school – as it is in OFSTED inspections and in virtually all media coverage – Parveen is quite right to think that schools with only a few ethnic minority children are 'better' schools. Schools and LEAs with high proportions of ethnic minority children regularly appear low in the tables, and so are judged to be 'worse' than other schools. A similar conclusion is offered as a commonsense notion by Honeyford when he writes about *the plight of white children* in schools with a majority of ethnic minority pupils. He is assuming, as many others have done, that standards will inevitably drop as the numbers of children speaking English as a second language in a school increase.

Anxious about the school her children were attending, Parveen decided to move them. She chose Leafylane, a primary school in a different authority, on the outskirts of a big city. However, the problems seemed to worsen, as she explains below:

01	Parveen:	.. and my brother didn't send them (his children) to any of these schools, he lives in Bradford as well .. but, he's sent his to Goldcrest .. private school .. so they've had the
05		basic foundation. But he's got five children, and he was paying a lot out .. but after that, they found the school in Leafylane and, he thought , well it's near, rather than going into the actual city. And because he'd found that, I
10		thought, well .. I wasn't happy with my schools

10   in Bradford, so that's why I transferred them over there. But we had a bit of problems with the headmaster as well, he was a bit racist and that, with one or two teachers and that. I

15   complained to them, to the authority, because they were through there, and you know .. you know .. the council, they sent some people .. a man over, anyway, to have a word with him.

20   They realised that there was nothing up there that was sort of, just, bilingual or anything representing other, you know, other cultures and things. So I think they've started to do that after the man came over. But there was a lot of racism within the children as well .. he [the headmaster] says, .. well you can't stop

25   that .. you know .. really racist comments..

At the second school, the family encounter what Parveen explicitly describes as racism (line 13). A man from 'the council' is called in to address the problems after Parveen makes a complaint. He seems to see the problem as a failure on the part of the school to acknowledge language and cultural diversity (lines 19-21). His proposed solution seems to be to put up displays. When I asked Parveen about this later, she confirmed that this was indeed what he suggested. She thought it an inadequate response to the problems. Her closing comments in the above extract only begin to touch on what she considers to be the real problems in the school. She went on to describe what she perceived as the endemic racism of the community surrounding Leafylane School, and how it was manifested in the behaviour of Anwar's classmates and their parents. Such deep-seated problems will not be satisfactorily addressed by displays acknowledging language diversity. The headteacher's reluctance to tackle such racism on a wider scale is understandable, if disappointing. Until Parveen and her family came along, institutional racism would hardly have ranked high on his agenda.

Conversation Two – an incident at Windyhill

After the experience at Leafylane, Anwar and his brothers Ejaz and Iftikhar were moved to a first school in Bradford, much nearer home that I call 'Windyhill'. But things did not always go smoothly here either. In another long conversation, Parveen described an incident where, again, she felt the teacher rebuffed her rights as a parent and caused her personal hurt:

01	Parveen:	.. because . again .. in Windyhill .. Mrs S., she were just so rude to me. It was the reason I took them to that school, it was Mrs. W., I think, she was the headmistress there before
05		Mrs. B. But apparently Mrs. B. was on leave, so there was really nobody there, because of her back problems, so she wasn't around. And .. erm .. I think it was Ejaz .. which one? .. I went in and told her that he could read, so
10		because I thought obviously you've got to negotiate and tell her beforehand, you know, because .. And she just turned round and she 1 goes. 'I .. am I the teacher .. or are you?'
	JC:	oh .. dear ..
15	Parveen:	you know .. I don't know what comments she made ..
	JC:	so this was when you .. so which year was he in then?
	Parveen:	I don't know whether it was him or Ejaz .. I
20		don't think he was in .. actually, no .. it was Ejaz or Iftikhar .. I'd gone in for them and told her, you know and she just, well, she just .. said, 'am I the teacher or you?' and she just looked at me like that. I just felt like .. I wanted
25		a hole, you know, to just take me in, I thought, you know, just look at the way she just answered me back, she was very rude. She was trying to say, 'you're nothing' ...

Parveen obviously found the teacher's comment personally wounding. The teacher's words, 'am I the teacher or you?' (line 13) indicate her need for a rigid demarcating of rôles and boundaries, reminiscent of Sharp and Green's (1975) argument that teachers need to set the agenda to which parents must comply. That Parveen is an ethnic minority parent no doubt reinforced the teacher's view. Parveen might be welcome to help out at social events and on school trips, but she is not expected to have knowledge and opinions about pedagogy.

The situation is compounded by the fact that Parveen was in the middle of training to be a teacher at the time. There are very few ethnic minority teachers in Bradford, as elsewhere in England, and even fewer women. There are, however, many classroom assistants and support assistants from ethnic minorities, usually women (as at Windyhill). They are subservient to classroom teachers in the school hierarchy. Ethnic minority teachers and students on teaching practice often talk about being mistaken in the classroom for such 'helpers' and feel justifiably upset at having their status as teachers or trainee teachers called into question. Some of them find this one obstacle too many to cope with and may give up teaching. Parveen is made of sterner stuff, but was nevertheless upset by the incident.

She goes on, with remarkable insight, to compare this experience with the way she was treated at Leafylane:

01	Parveen:	and that really .. that really put me off .. so that's the reason I thought .. right .. and I already think they're not doing anything anyway. I thought, right I'll move them .. and
05		so .. and I didn't find racism in there. I'm not talking about racism. It was just her attitude towards me, and I thought if that's her attitude, what's she going to do for my son? And there was no headmistress to complain to or
10		anything, but I did go in to Miss G. .. oh .. I think. Tears just came, I was so upset that she could have said that to me.

Parveen's analysis illustrates how she perceives herself in the context. As we can see from what she says in line 05, she does not define what happens at Windyhill as *racist*. She sees the teacher's attack on her as personal and thus potentially more wounding. When we discussed this later, she agreed with this view. She described the teacher's response as '*undermining*' her. She is basing this judgement partly on other cues she picked up during the interaction such as the teacher's body language. In contrast, she was adamant that what went on at Leafylane was racist, but this did not seem to affect her so personally.

In a later conversation, she agreed with this analysis of the two incidents. She described herself as being *the other* at Leafylane, the one who was *multicultural* where everyone else at the school was not. In the apparently monocultural school setting, Parveen seemed clear about her outsider rôle. She did not, and did not want to, belong in this community. She did not want anything more from it than a 'good' education for her sons.

At Windyhill, however, her position is different. The school is part of a diverse community. Parveen lives near the school. The teacher is known to many other parents. She has developed ways of communicating with parents and children from a range of social and cultural contexts. Parveen interprets the response as personally excluding her from a community of which she feels she is a rightful member. Her differing responses to the incidents also reveal the ways in which external factors can so strongly influence what happens in classrooms. At Leafylane, Parveen hoped for no more than a 'good' education for her sons. This was not possible because of the ways community attitudes invaded the classroom, influencing the teachers' attitudes and the teachers' and children's behaviour. Parveen did not want to be included in this community whereas at Windyhill she assumed that she would be included in discussions about her son's education partly because of her status as a member of the community. It hurt her to feel excluded.

By the end of Year Six, Anwar had attended five or six different schools. His parents, increasingly frustrated with the system, decided to move him into a private school where his brothers were already pupils. It was a school run on traditional lines with formal pedagogy and virtually no recognition of language and cultural diversity. Despite this, Parveen was happy with the school, believing that it was clear about its aims and goals, and that it would help her sons to achieve good exam results. The rest she could do at home. Her confidence in the private school system matches findings reported by Nieto (1999) about the success of African American pupils in Catholic schools in America. Again, there are ironic echoes of Honeyford here. Parveen was happy that Anwar's new school would provide him with the kind of 'good education' which she considered he needed to succeed. In broad terms, that education was very similar to the one Honeyford wrote about as upholding the best values of 'British culture'.

On the surface, Parveen's attitude seems to contradict what I have been saying about the good schools being the ones which recognise and value children's different language and cultural experiences. Her attitude is not uncommon – I have heard it expressed by many Asian parents. The hope that their children will grow up 'better' than they are is a powerful parental aspiration, especially if the parents themselves have struggled. In the past, 'English' parents – such as mine – from backgrounds where education was not really a strong element of the culture were keen for their children to 'get on' and go to university. I was the first in my family to do so, and in the process I took on a culture and a language that was largely alien to my parents. I think they were quite proud of this but it created a gap between us which has never really been bridged. Perhaps this is inevitable as each generation becomes independent from the previous one, but it is sad if the gap becomes too wide ever to be crossed – and this is the risk that Parveen is taking.

I am not suggesting that Parveen is representative of 'Asian' parents, but her ability to analyse the issues means that she has important things to say which help us to understand their complexity. She is acutely aware, because of her personal experience and because she is a bilingual teacher from an ethnic minority, of the problems which beset many ethnic minority children within the education system. If Anwar and his brothers continue to succeed in school, his mother's ability to analyse the problems and contradictions presented by the system and to make her choices accordingly will be a strong contributing factor.

SUMMARY OF KEY ISSUES

In this chapter, I have discussed the children's home and family experiences and considered how they influence their achievement in school. I have tried to analyse them to show how they might help the children to succeed in school. Through the words of one of the parents, I have shown some of the dilemmas ethnic minority parents face in attempting to involve themselves in their children's education. These are some of the main points:

- The children's families are closely-knit and provide strong support for their schooling

- The range and diversity of the children's home language and cultural experiences is extensive and they are able to discuss them confidently

- The children (and their parents) have a clear sense of their cultural identity and of belonging to different cultures from the mainstream

- The potentially positive effects of these experiences on children's school achievement need to be carefully considered

- Parents show a strong sense of the value of maintaining heritage languages and cultures within family and community contexts

- At the same time, they recognise the need to become proficient in English and to work hard in school in order to succeed in the mainstream school system and in later life

- Parents who aspire for their children to succeed have to somehow reconcile the contradictions entailed in this – in succeeding, their children are likely, in some ways, to become strangers to them

- Parents recognise the importance of maintaining effective communication with their children's teachers, but are more likely than ethnic majority parents to face misunderstanding

- When communication goes wrong, the effects can be deep and intensely harmful.

4

THE CHILDREN LEARNING AT SCHOOL: TALKING AND LEARNING IN PRIMARY CLASSROOMS

Chapters Two and Three described the children's home and community contexts. In this chapter and the next, I focus more closely on their schools and their conversations with their teachers.

Teachers talking

Collaborative talk is a key way in which learning is mediated in primary classrooms. Some of the best opportunities for children to engage in such talk with each other can arise in groupwork and problem-solving activities which enable them to take part in discussions. Such activities are not always easy to organise and carry out effectively. Teachers often feel disappointed because they find that children cannot always manage discussions by themselves. When they intervene to try to help things along, the nature of the activity can change – the children's attention becomes focused on the teacher and not on each other. Instead of actively seeking to explore for themselves what they are learning, they tend to wait until the teacher gives them the right answer.

Part of the problem is that children may not know what is involved in taking part in collaborative talk, having never heard it as part of their everyday experience. It is not a 'natural' way of talking, in the way that a personal conversation between adult and child, or children together is. It is difficult to construct a truly collaborative discussion – how many of us as adults can actually manage to do it? Just as children need to be taught how to construct a piece of writing, they need to be shown how to construct a discussion. They need opportunities to learn about the vocabulary, grammar and text organisation of discussions, just as they learn about the word, sentence and text level features of a written story, report or piece of persuasive writing.

The teachers in the first school recognised the value and importance of collaborative talk in their classroom and both saw it as an important part of the children's learning experiences. They frequently organised whole class discussions, where the teacher sat on a low chair facing the children on the carpet. As part of the arrangements for their jobshare, the teachers had a shared hour of liaison time on Wednesday afternoons. They used part of this time for a session of collaborative talk which involved them both together with the children. Sandra was in charge of the class on Wednesdays and Janet came to school in the afternoon for the liaison time. Both would sit with the whole class on the carpet for about half an hour at the end of the day, initiating a three-way conversation about the work the class had been doing recently and their plans about what to do next. The children took an active part in this, answering questions and offering detail and comment about the work they had been doing since Janet was last in school at the end of the previous week. They often provided her with information that she genuinely did not know, as she explained:

> ... I really don't know what they've done some of the time, I mean, I might've got a gist 'cos I, you know. I know what's happening at the beginning of the week with a general idea and, then, Sandra's a general idea of what I'll be doing at the end of the week, but I do, you know you do genuinely go in there and not know exactly what they've done, I mean sometimes I don't understand some of the things that they've done, and I've got to say, well, can you explain that a bit more 'cos I'm not quite sure what you mean, and I'm not just saying that ...

Thus individual children are placed, even if only briefly, in the rôle of teacher, as the person who has the knowledge. There is a need for authentic negotiation between teacher and learner. Janet and Sandra are doing something very unusual for primary teachers in openly accepting that the children know something that they do not. It changes the classroom culture quite a bit.

Bruner (1996) reports examples of schools which have set up 'mutual communities' where teachers and learners 'help each other get the lay of the land and the hang of the job' through a division of labour and the sharing of clear rôles. He suggests that such practices have benefits for the learners' self-confidence and growing independence. Similarly, Wells and Chang-Wells (1992) talk about the value of 'sharing sessions' in primary classrooms where teachers and children learn from each other. The Wednesday afternoon three-way conversations seemed to be an event of this kind and reaped similar benefits. That the children were hearing two adults talking to each other at length and in a particular way was a further advantage. Each teacher was learning from the other and from the children. It is rare for children in primary classrooms to hear two adults talking to each other as equals, informing each other about topics which are quite familiar to the children themselves. Usually, when two or more adults are present in a classroom, one is in some way in charge of the others. They are expected to act out this power relationship with each other, no matter how politely and sensitively, so the interaction is not collaborative in the ways that we hope children's discussions among themselves will be. Participating on an equal power basis in the three-way conversations meant that the *negotiation* was much more strongly apparent in their talk than is usually the case.

Three extracts from one Wednesday afternoon conversation will show what I mean. They illustrate how the teachers and children worked together to construct a classroom culture. This conversation was one of many I recorded. Many of the children had been members of the class for almost 18 months, so they knew what was expected of them and were expert actors in their respective rôles. The whole conversation lasted about 30 minutes, ranging over a variety of topics and including responses from most of the children. The support assistant who was present was included at one point when Sandra asked her to show the class a book of the children's writing she had been putting together. I was brought in at the end when the teachers asked if I would like the children to sing their new song for me.

The extracts I have chosen provide evidence of some of the distinctive features of the ways the teachers and children 'negotiate the world' (Bruner, 1996) to create joint cultures in their classroom. Through their interaction, they are answering the three questions I mentioned in Chapter One which provide the main framework of the culture of the classroom:

- What are we learning?
- How are we learning it?
- Why are we learning it?

Extract One – What are we learning? New beginnings

This conversation took place in January, soon after the children had returned to school after the Christmas holidays. Janet had begun some RE work the previous week related to the New Year and the way 'new beginnings' featured in the children's lives. Sandra had continued this at the start of the week in which the conversation happened. This extract begins where Sandra has just asked the children to explain to Janet what they have been doing since the previous Friday when Janet had last been in the class (ie three teaching days ago). Janet asks a general question to start the conversation going:

01	Janet:	what did you do about new beginnings?
	Sandra:	Shaheen
	Shaheen:	we had to write ...the first thing ... we had to think of the title for the beginning things, then
05		we had to think of some things that we wrote about ... after that we had to work in twos with a book and write
	Sandra:	mmm ... we chose a new beginning and wrote about it ... so what sort of things did people write about? ... Rehana
10	Rehana:	miss ... like when we had a new baby brother or sister, or when ... mm ... a wedding
	Sandra:	new babies in the house or a wedding
	Janet:	wedding ... mm

15	Sandra:	anything else ... Tommy, come on, quickly have a little think and see if you can think of another new beginning. Andy, what did you write about?
	Andy:	moving
20	Sandra:	moving house, that's another new beginning, isn't it? Joe?
	Joe:	a birthday
	Sandra:	birthdays ... we did write a little bit about birthdays
	Janet:	that's right, isn't it?
25	Sandra:	because that's the beginning of a new year, isn't it, yes?
	Janet:	oh yes, that's right

Janet and Sandra often set up different patterns of response to each other and to the children. Here, they repeat what a child says in order to reinforce its appropriacy. This happens four times in the short extract above, at lines 07, 13, 19 and 22. The response sometimes goes further than simple repetition: when a child's answer has some potential for developing ideas about what constitute 'new beginnings', Sandra re-phrases it, selecting the features which suit her purposes. She does this with Shaheen's contribution (lines 03-06). For Shaheen, the important point seems to be not the knowledge content of the activity but the fact that the children had to do some writing. Shaheen takes Janet's question, 'What did you do...?' as an invitation to talk about the process of writing, not about the content of her own piece of writing. Her words 'the beginning things' suggest that she is a bit vague about what precisely she had to write about – it is the act of writing which is more significant to her. She answers what is possibly a 'what are we learning?' question more in terms of 'how are we learning it?'

At lines 08-09, Sandra acknowledges this. She repeats slowly what Shaheen has said, then re-phrases Janet's original question, so ensuring that Shaheen's suggestion does not disappear as later contributions from other children do. In fact, Sandra refers to writing several times again in the next few minutes – twice more in this short extract (lines 16 and 22), adjusting the direction of the conversation to accommodate Shaheen's concerns into the activity of thinking about new beginnings. Through her talk, Sandra is also openly negotiating what kind of activity writing is in this classroom for the children.

Another pattern we can see in the above extract involves Sandra and Janet without the children. They talk to each other to affirm what each has said and to show the children that they agree about what counts as relevant knowledge for the topic. This happens twice in the above extract, at lines 12-15 and again at lines 22-25. These affirming comments do not add anything to the content of the talk or change its direction. They are very much about the 'how' of learning in this case. They serve the important function in constructing cultures of showing the children that both teachers agree about what constitutes appropriate content in this particular context, and how to talk about it.

A few seconds further on, Shabana brings up the topic of driving lessons, and we see that the teachers handle it differently from the earlier topics:

01	Sandra:	yes, we've mentioned weddings ... emm ... Shabana
	Shabana:	driving lessons
	Sandra:	well, no, I don't think that any of you wrote about that. But we did say that when you
05		passed your driving test
	Janet:	oh, yes
	Sandra:	it was a new beginning, wasn't it ... yes
	Janet:	it's a new type of life, isn't it
10	Sandra:	yes
	Janet:	if you are able to get yourself about
	Sandra:	yes
	Janet:	yes, that's right, Shabana . Well done
	Sandra:	but these children were writing about things
15		that happened to them

Janet:	yes, to them
Sandra:	so they can ... er ... Peter?
Peter:	passing your driving test
Janet:	that's just what Shabana said
20 Sandra:	we'll have one more

At first, Sandra appears to reject Shabana's contribution, then she softens this by referring back to an earlier part of the discussion where passing the driving test was mentioned. Janet then picks up the theme and elaborates it. She actually ends by affirming Shabana's contribution (line 13). Sandra then goes on to add a new factor to the context (lines 14-15): the children were to write about things which had happened to them. Janet immediately agrees with this (line 16). There is genuine negotiation here. In a very short space, the two teachers have shown the children that you can disagree about something but still remain friends. Janet is happy to allow her view of the appropriacy of a particular piece of knowledge – that driving lessons are a new beginning – to be modified by Sandra through the introduction of a new condition, that the children were asked to choose events which had happened to them personally. In addition, Shabana, a quiet child who seldom participated much in whole-class discussions, has been given a positive response even though what she said was not strictly relevant. When Peter refers to the topic again, however (line 18), Janet quickly gives him a clear message that it is now not an acceptable one. This is an example of the two teachers constructing together through their talk a framework for the children to operate within while at the same time responding sensitively to the different needs of the children. They each seem to know what the other is thinking.

Extract Two – How are we learning it? Doing PE

The class had had a PE lesson in the hall with Sandra earlier in the afternoon. She described to Janet how well the children had worked to put the apparatus away after the lesson and then awarded the class a marble in the jar as a prize for their good behaviour. Twenty marbles in the jar and there would be a class treat. Sandra then initiated a conversation about putting the equipment away:

01	Sandra:	who can remember how long it took to put the apparatus away? I actually timed them. Can you remember, Shafqat?
	Shafqat:	three o'clock
05	Sandra:	three ... ?
	Ch. tog:	three minutes
	Janet:	well done. Three minutes? goodness me, that's very quick, isn't it?
10	Sandra:	it's very quick. I was very, very impressed. We didn't get the big frame out, but we got everything else out
	Janet:	and that takes quite a while, doesn't it, to organise?
	Sandra:	well it does, yes
15	Janet:	they've done really well
	Sandra:	so we've ... they've got a few ideas about why we managed to do it so quickly
	Janet:	mmm ...
20	Sandra:	would you like to just tell Mrs. T. why we thought we had done it so quickly? yes, Bushra?
	Bushra:	miss, because we were sitting nicely near the wall
25	Sandra:	right, people were sitting sensibly, so there was nobody in the way, right
	Janet:	when children are trying to put apparatus away, that's very sensible, isn't it?
	Sandra:	Harpreet?
	Harpreet:	people were listening
30	Sandra:	people were listening
	Janet:	good

| | Sandra: | it used to happen that I had to tell children over and over again, but today, they listened and they did it straight away |

35   Janet: well done

(the children give more reasons why they put the apparatus away so quickly)

Sandra: One more reason ... Qasar?

Qasar: miss, when they were putting the apparatus away, they were doing it sensibly

40   Sandra: they were doing it sensibly, they were working together, weren't they? So that meant that everything was done quite quickly but it was done safely, very good

Janet: well that was really good, I certainly think that they deserve a marble in the jar for that, Miss
45   S. I wonder how many we've got

Sandra makes it clear that managing the PE equipment is an important part of the lesson. She wants to emphasise certain issues of safety, but she also wants the children to learn about good behaviour in a more general way. She expects the children to do what they are asked, and also to be able to talk about it. The two teachers and the children take on definite rôles in this extract. Sandra's rôle is to inform Janet about what happened, which she does in lines 01-02, 09-011, 16-17, 24-25, 32-34 and 39-42 and Janet's rôle is to affirm it: this is virtually all she does here. The children's rôle is to provide the teachers with evidence that they have understood the message of *safety* (despite the fact that Sandra tends to emphasise the notion of *speed*). They all answer Sandra's questions in terms of careful behaviour, using the words and phrases which they have no doubt heard their teachers use at different times: *sitting nicely; listening; doing it sensibly*, and even echoing their stress and intonation, as can be heard on the tape.

Putting the PE equipment away is established as a collaborative activity for which everyone shares responsibility. The ways in which it should be done are clearly established in the language which Sandra uses and which the children echo. The collaboration goes beyond this. Janet's closing remark about the marbles in the jar establishes that collecting rewards for good behaviour is another collaborative activity. The teachers even have a part to play in this, as Janet's use of the pronoun *we* in the last line above indicates. Someone was sent off to count the marbles. Sandra proudly announced the result to the class a few minutes later, 'Nineteen! So we just need one more, and then we'll get a class reward!'

Extract Three – Why are we learning it? A new song

During Sandra's time with the class, they had a weekly singing lesson with a Mr. S., a peripatetic pianist. In this particular week, they had started learning a new song, *doh – a deer* (from *The Sound of Music*). Sandra invites the children to tell Janet about it.

01	Sandra:	why did Mr S. think that would be a good song for us to learn because it was his idea, he had it already there for us, he was very helpful

(three children make different guesses, then...)

	Janet:	Gillian's had her hand up quite a long time
05	Sandra:	Gillian
	Gillian:	because it's different ways of saying things
	Sandra:	no, no it's not different ways of saying things , no ... Bushra?
	Bushra:	it's in different languages
10	Sandra:	no, it's not in different languages ...
	Janet:	it's a good idea, though, isn't it?
	Sandra:	I was just saying last week that Mrs. J. brought us that old Christmas card
	Janet:	that's beautiful, isn't it?
15	Sandra:	because she knew that this class liked to think about different languages
	Janet:	right
	Sandra:	somebody sent the card to her, but she thought that we might like to keep it in our classroom

20	Janet:	yes, definitely, I saw that last week
	Sandra:	we are interested in different languages, but that ... er ... that isn't why we are doing that song, Nahida?
	Nahida:	miss is it because it'll make us better singers?
25	Sandra:	well, I'm sure it will
	Janet:	oh ... mmm ...
	Sandra:	I'm sure it will
	Janet:	she's almost on the right track, isn't she?

Sandra's initial question reinforces for the children the idea that they do things at school for particular purposes and that the teachers know what these are, though the children may not. The children offer several reasons of their own for learning the song which all have validity in terms of the kind of culture Sandra and Janet are trying to develop in the classroom. Gillian's comment comes from her awareness of ways the children are encouraged to widen their vocabularies in different activities. She uses a phrase, 'different ways of saying', which Sandra and Janet sometimes use in explaining and discussing vocabulary and word meaning with the children. Bushra's idea comes from her sense that different languages are a valid topic for classroom discussion. In this classroom they certainly are – on my first visit, one little boy met me at the door and asked me how many languages I spoke. Sandra immediately confirms this with the example of the Christmas card given to the class by another member of staff in the school and with her definitive statement in line 15. Then Nahida offers a suggestion (line 24) which reveals her understanding of the whole purpose for going to school at all (to 'be able to do things better'), and her faith in the powers of Mr. S. Once again, Janet affirms her idea and hints at the 'official' reason for learning the song.

The guessing continues – the children are enjoying the game. It is interesting how no child repeats what another has already said. They keep trying out new ideas. Here are the closing turns to this part of the conversation and almost to the whole conversation as a whole, which ends immediately afterwards with a performance of the song to the great satisfaction of all:

01	Anwar:	miss, is it because it came from the Caribbean?
	Sandra:	no, it doesn't, but it would be nice if we could find a song from the Caribbean to learn, wouldn't it, Anwar? We have been listening to some Caribbean music
05		
	Yasmin:	yeah, miss, it were like a steel band
	Sandra:	a steel band, yes, we liked that ... in fact , when you go for your dinner, I've been listening to it
	Janet:	oh yes (laughter)
10	Sandra:	I'm enjoying that
	Janet:	it's nice music, isn't it?
	Sandra:	Suzanne
	Suzanne:	miss, because it's nice and 'joyable
	Sandra:	well it is a nice enjoyable song, isn't it. Suzanne?
15		
	Sandra:	er ... that's not the reason, though it is a nice enjoyable song, it's because each of the different words, each of the notes gets higher and higher and higher

(several children join in, repeating 'higher', and make a hubbub of noise)

20	Sandra:	and, hang on, I think Nahida might have got it now, Nahida, what did you say?
	Nahida:	miss, we were learning about ... about pitch
	Sandra:	OK so that's our new song

Anwar's suggestion is appropriate because the class has been studying St. Lucia, a National Curriculum topic. Janet and Sandra take the opportunity to reinforce the positive aspects of this. Suzanne's idea mirrors Nahida's earlier one in its awareness of the possible reasons for which things can be done in schools. But the game has to end sometime so Sandra throws in a few clues, hoping the children will remember the word she gave them the day before when they were learning the song. At last she is rewarded by Nahida's answer in line 22. The official reason for learning the song is finally identified and labelled to the manifest satisfaction of the teachers.

These examples of the talk of two skilled primary teachers with their pupils reveal for us some of the features which Sandra and Janet consider to be important in classroom learning – in other words their theories about teaching and learning. They give us evidence for both the teachers' and the children's beliefs about what is important for effective learning. They show how each group negotiates with the other to construct a joint culture of learning. In these extracts the teachers do most of the talking, but they do not always play the dominant rôle. There is considerable evidence at various points of ways in which the children appropriate their teachers' discourses, taking the words out of their mouths, so to speak, to negotiate their own meanings.

Sandra and Janet are constructing a joint culture of learning with the children they are teaching. It concerns not just the transaction of knowledge but also the individual and community values they consider important such as sharing with each other, working together, taking care of each other's possessions and so on. They are demonstrating that successful learning is a result of negotiation and that all participants share responsibility for the successful outcome of the negotiation. Also, they begin to reveal the powerful cognitive benefits to be gained from making the processes of negotiation explicit in the classroom interaction. The teachers are providing a model for the children of the things that can be done with talk. Sandra herself acknowledged this in a conversation I had with her later on, when she talked about the value for the children of hearing two adults talking which provided them with a rôle model for talking in the same way as 'you would like them to see you sitting reading'.

Children talking: conversations about science in the first school

This section presents some extracts from an activity I conducted with a small group of children, the same girls we heard talking in Chapter Three about weddings and such matters. We see how the girls seem to have picked up from their teachers some of the features of collaborative talk discussed in the last section. Also I think the extracts show that the children are influenced by the kind of community-constructed talk that goes on in their homes, also discussed in Chapter Three. By comparing what they said with what they wrote in this activity, I show how the talk gave them greater opportunity to learn about the science concepts which were the learning objectives of the activity than the writing did.

The activity took place when the children were almost at the end of Year 4. It was science-based, an investigation to find out which of a set of five balls would bounce the highest. The teachers in the middle school to which the children were transferring had asked the first school teachers to do it so they would have some evidence of the children's understanding of science. One condition was that it should be carried out without adult direction. When I got to the class on the Wednesday afternoon, only three girls had not done the task and the teacher asked me to go through it with them. It was not altogether easy to avoid directing at the same time as supervising and trying to make sure that the balls did not bounce too far! The girls knew what the activity entailed as they had seen other children doing it earlier in the week. I told them I was going to be the observer but they kept drawing me in. My presence and the interventions I made obviously changed their engagement with the task. For a start, it kept the children far more focused, and I thought this was appropriate. I tried not to make my interventions directive, but to give the children space to work out how to do things for themselves.

The activity lasted for about an hour and the talk was virtually continual throughout. The transcript of the audiotape covers about twenty pages of text. The children talked about many things as well as the science they were supposed to be doing. Some of the topics that came up in their conversation, most of them typical of nine-year old girls, were:

• swimming
• teletubbies
• make-up
• the number of countries we had visited between us
• whether speaking Punjabi would be acceptable in middle school

When they did get to the science, much of what the children said concerned the 'what', 'how' and 'why' of what they were learning, as the extracts I have chosen illustrate. My analysis has close parallels with the approach followed by Gibbons (1998) in her exposition of the social elements of learning a science topic among 9- and 10- year old bilingual children in Australia.

Extract One – What are we learning? The children constructing knowledge

At the point where this extract starts, the children are about to write their predictions on the sheets given to them by their teacher (you can see an example on page 84) before they carry out the investigation. To help them make their choices, we discuss the different properties of the balls:

01	JC:	that's quite, what would you say? No, don't bounce them ... I said, don't bounce them ... what would you say was the difference between that one and that one?
05	Parveen:	miss, more air in ... it's got more air in
	Rehana:	this is harder
	JC:	that's a bit harder, that's a bit softer
	Rehana:	miss, this has got holes in it ...
	JC:	that's got holes in it, but it's actually ... it's very ...
10	Ch. tog:	hard
	JC:	hard, isn't it? and it's actually ...
	Parveen:	smaller
	JC:	smaller ... what about that one?
	Parveen:	that's soft ...
15	JC:	that's very soft, yes. So, what do you think, then? ... Let's put them all here, put them all over here. What do you think then, we've got ... hard ... hardness and softness, we've got size.
20	Rehana:	medium
	JC:	yes, we've got a small one, a medium one, we've got big ones
	Nahida:	soft

Rehana:	miss, the air, this one, the air, this one will
25	bounce most, it's going to be ...

JC:	now, why do you think that one will bounce the highest?

Rehana:	because there's more air in it

I begin the discussion about the balls by introducing the theme of *differences*. My hope is that the children will identify the ways in which the balls look and feel different. However, Parveen (line 05) immediately catches on to the idea of air in the balls. Because I intervene again (old habits die hard!), Parveen's idea is left and we go back to talking about size, hardness and so on. The children willingly join in with this, using words such as *hard, smaller, big, little, medium, soft*. They are happy to supply the right words to make my conversation work. But their real interest is in choosing the ball they think will bounce the highest, so that *their* contest can begin.

The discussion about size and hardness does not seem to offer the children what they are looking for, so Rehana returns to the theme of *air* in line 24, linking it directly with bouncing. The connection between air and bouncing was something which had not occurred to me but it was clearly important to the children. Nahida subsequently offered it in writing as grounds for her prediction on her report sheet. When each chooses the ball they think will bounce the highest, it is the idea of air which holds them:

01	Nahida:	miss, I pick this one
	Parveen:	no, I pick that one
	JC:	listen to what Rehana says ... Rehana said she thought this one will bounce the highest ...
05	Parveen:	why ...
	JC:	it might ... because it's got ...
	Nahida:	more air
	Rehana:	more air
	JC:	air in it. OK

10   Parveen: ... miss, I think the spongy one because it hasn't got any air in at all

       JC: you think the spongy one, because

       Parveen: yeah, Miss

       JC: it'll ... it hasn't got any air in ...

It is easy to see why the children seized on the idea of air in the balls. There is a powerful intuitive connection between air and *bouncing*. After all, footballs bounce higher when they are fully inflated than when they are not. Compelling evidence was to hand in the investigation – one of the balls had a leak and when someone squeezed the air out of it, it would not bounce at all. It seems to me that they are participating in the kind of valuable 'exploratory talk' discussed by Mercer *et al* (1999) where 'reasoning is visible'. They are confidently handling the dynamics of the kind of discussion expected to take place as part of a scientific investigation. They are making 'personal sense', in Driver *et al*'s terms (1998), of the *validated* knowledge of science. We could almost claim that the children have constructed a viable scientific hypothesis and are exploring its possibilities. Though their hypothesis is wrong in the sense that it will not lead them to the scientifically validated knowledge about the factors which influence bouncing, this hardly matters. The evidence provided by their talk shows that they can engage in the processes of analytic thinking about the conditions for bouncing. It demonstrates clearly their growing control over the process skills discussed by Harlen (1996) as important in the constructivist model of learning in science incorporated into the National Curriculum. It also provides an example of the way the children have developed the capacity to use talk as a situated resource for their learning. One reason they can do this is that they have participated in sustained interactions with and between their teachers and have had the opportunity to go on to co-construct new texts for themselves.

When I showed the teachers the transcript of the children's science conversation, they were surprised at the length and complexity of their discussions. They were also impressed at the understanding of scientific concepts the talk revealed. They pointed out, however, that as class teachers they would not be able to devote as much time as I had done to a small group of children during a typical afternoon in the classroom.

They saw that this meant they missed valuable opportunities to appreciate the sophisticated nature of the children's thinking. They also contrasted the quality of the evidence of conceptual understanding shown by the children's talk compared with their written responses, which was all that the middle school teachers would have with which to assess the children's science understanding. Here is an example of the response sheet:

My Science Investigation

Which ball bounces the highest.

This is what I think will happen (Prediction)

I think the yellow, Spungie, Small, soft ball bounces the highest.

Because it has no air in it.

This is what I am going to do

I am going to use a long ruler. Somebody has to hold it. Then some one bounses the ruler a ball. Then mark it with with a chalk. The ball has to be thrown from the same height.

The children found it difficult to complete. At one point during the writing up, Yasmin read out loud the sentence, *This is what I found out* on the sheet, then turned to me and asked, 'Miss, what did I find out?' to which Nahida replied, 'to use your brain'.

Extract Two – How are we learning it? Carrying out a 'fair test'

There was a box on the recording sheet where the children had to write an explanation of how they would make their test 'fair'. We discussed this before beginning the practical work and the children wrote down their suggestions. This extract shows part of the discussion about making sure the test is fair:

01	JC:	yes, so you've got to decide the same way you drop one ball, you've got to drop all of the balls, haven't you? and that will help to answer
05		this question, 'this is how I will make my test fair'
	Rehana:	fair, I know how to make it fair
	JC:	yes
	Rehana:	with the ruler, if you hold it like that ...
	JC:	yes
10	Rehana:	move it with your hand you've got to ... and I'll tell you summat else, you've got to bounce it from the same height
	Yasmin:	do it from the same height
	Nahida:	same height
15	JC:	why is it important to have a fair test?
	Nahida:	because like, if the other ball, and they bounce it in a different way, and then ... the other balls won't bounce like that, this way, bouncing like that
20	JC:	yes, so that would be unfair, and what would happen to your results then? what will your results? ...

	Nahida:	they will be different
25	JC:	your results would be different for each one, and you won't, you won't have actually ...
	Yasmin:	yeah, somebody will not be telling the truth
25	JC:	yes, so you won't have actually found out which ball bounces the highest, will you?
	Rehana:	that's important ... we've got to find that out
30	JC:	yes, yes, so can you write now, can you write down what you're going to do, and then write the bit about the fair test, then we'll go and do it

We began discussing the ways the children could bounce the balls and the idea that they would have to try to bounce them all in the same way in order to make the test fair. The children all had ideas about what conducting a fair test entailed. Rehana linked it with holding the ruler straight (line 08) and bouncing the balls from the same height (line 12). Yasmin thought it was about 'telling the truth' (line 26). By observing the ways they behaved when we proceeded to the practical part of the task, I had no doubt that the children genuinely tried to perform the actions they had been talking about. They found it difficult at times because of their lack of experience and limited physical dexterity as nine-year olds, but they knew what scientists were expected to do and they relished the opportunity to behave like scientists. They also talked like scientists much of the time, using linguistic forms and vocabulary they would not have used in their everyday conversations. Not only were they jointly constructing knowledge, they were beginning to take ownership of the kinds of language which mediated that knowledge for them.

The children bounced each ball once and marked with a piece of chalk where it reached on a metre ruler held upright. One of them also wrote the heights on a piece of paper. Then they decided that they should do it all again. I asked them why and the following interaction ensued:

01	JC:	why do you think you should do it one more time?

	Rehana:	miss ...
	Yasmin:	miss, because to make sure it's right
	JC:	to make sure
05	Yasmin:	'cos no chalk this time
	JC:	mm-mm . so what are you going to do this time, use a different coloured chalk?
	Yasmin:	are we gonna ... we gonna ... to put the mark on again?
10	JC:	do you think that'll be a good idea
	Yasmin:	yeah
	Rehana:	to make sure it is on that mark, miss
	JC:	yes, OK
	Rehana:	so which one was the first one to do?

Rehana is clear (line 12) that what they need to do is check that the chalk marks on the ruler are correct. When they did the second bounces and found that the balls reached different heights from the first, the scribe crossed out the first heights she had written on the piece of paper. It ended up looking like this:

The notion of a fair test seems to mean to the children that they should do everything as carefully and accurately as possible in order to get the 'right' answer. That is the point of it all, as far as they are concerned. This is not quite the 'validated' National Curriculum definition of a fair test, though we have seen that the children have clearly captured the notion of there being separate factors involved in successfully carrying out a fair test. But their own understanding of the purpose for conducting science investigations seems to be dominated by the need to find the right answer. This answer exists somewhere, and it is their task to seek it out. It seems to me that this is a perceptive viewpoint on the way science is often carried out in schools. As Edwards and Mercer showed (1987), 'discovery approaches' to learning are not always what they claim to be. Edwards and Mercer observed how teachers tried hard to set up discovery approaches in their classrooms but how – once set up – they could only allow the children to 'discover' through the activities what they (the teachers) needed them to. They could not afford to allow them to pursue lines of investigation which they knew would not lead them to the results required for successful completion of the task according to the curriculum.

Extract Three – Why are we learning it? The second bounce

There is also evidence from comments the children make throughout the whole conversation that they had their own view of why they were doing the science task, appearing to see the investigation as a competition in which they have a strong personal investment. For example, at one point, Nahida says of the balls, 'Which one's going to win?' When about to bounce one of the balls, Rehana says, 'Ready, steady, go...' and after the bounce, Nahida asks the others, 'Did you vote for that one?' When I try to encourage the children to speculate on why their results for the first and second bounces are different, a quarrel breaks out:

01   JC: do you think, was it wrong the first time?

      Yasmin: I think she's bouncing them differently

      JC: I think there's maybe something ... yes ...

      Rehana: (*indignantly*) miss, I just bounce em like that,
05   and it goes up to there

	JC:	yes, but even if you try your hardest, you might be doing ...
	Rehana:	(*upset*) miss, this time I'm going to ...
10	Yasmin:	some ... she can be bouncing like that (*demonstrating*), so that's why they go a bit lower, and some she can be bouncing like that (*demonstrating*) ...
	JC:	yes, so ...
	Yasmin:	maybe, it will go a little bit higher ...
15	JC:	can you just hold the balls, alright
	Rehana:	maybe it's you, Yasmin, marking them wrong
	JC:	Rehana, can you think about it? it's not that it's ...
	Nahida:	yeah ...
20	JC:	Nahida, can you listen, it's not that it's right or wrong, but this is why we thought maybe you've got to do it more than once because you might find that they're all different or you might find that ...
	Yasmin:	every time ...
25	Rehana:	miss, it's me or her, it's me bouncing em wrong, or it's her ... holding the ruler wrong ...

The written transcript does not fully capture the emotions unleashed at this point in the activity. At line 15, Rehana has thrown the balls on the floor behind me and Nahida is making faces at her, hence my attempts to keep order. There is clearly much at stake here for the children. Rehana feels she is being accused of great misdemeanours and Nahida sees the chance to stir things up. Yasmin takes no part in the argument, making comments (lines 02, 09-11, 14, and 24) which are unrelated. Through all the drama, she continues speculating in a sustained way on the reasons for the differences between the first and second bounces. If you read her four turns in the conversation one after the other, you will see that they form a connected sentence which shows grammatical and conceptual complexity and sophistication. Her tone remains calm throughout the whole conversation. She carries on regardless of the fracas caused by the other two because Rehana has taken her suggestion about the differences in the bounces as an attack on her ball bouncing skills. By the end of this extract, it was becoming difficult to hear much at all on the tape because of the force of Rehana's righteous indignation.

For the children, the science task has the excitement of a game and its completion the thrill of victory or the chagrin of defeat. They have subverted the official definition of a 'fair test' to suit their own purposes of setting up an exciting competition, skilfully using many of the processes of negotiation through talk which underpin successful science learning and learning in general. Even Rehana, despite her emotional outburst, is observing, speculating, hypothesising and drawing conclusions, all of which provides evidence that she is operating at a high level of skill within the academic genre of science.

A different view of success: a science lesson in Year Six

Rehana, Nahida and Yasmin were still together in class when they reached Year Six in the middle school, but things had changed. The class had eleven different teachers in the course of a week and their timetable was divided into twenty lessons (four each day) with eleven different subjects. They had two lessons of science each week, each lasting an hour and ten minutes, taught by different teachers. With the permission of the teachers, I observed some of these lessons and extracts from the transcript of one of the lessons follow. By this time, Key Stage Two SATs are drawing near and the pressure is on to make sure the school meets its targets. I have selected only one lesson from the many I observed in the middle school, mainly to try to show some contrasts in the style of lessons in first and middle schools. I do not wish to imply a judgement or suggest that there were no lessons in the middle school where collaborative talk was a strong feature. There were some, though the kind of lesson presented here was much more common. It seemed that the middle school teachers felt the need to exercise much greater control over the children's learning than the first school teachers did. Classrooms were generally much quieter and more orderly. The children followed routines obediently but did not seem to be personally involved in what they were doing. When I asked them about their lessons, they generally answered in terms of procedures and routines, rather than ideas and content.

There were 28 children present in the lesson described here. The week before, the whole class had made a visit to a science museum where they observed displays and experiments to do with heating and cooling. The content of the lesson centred on the effects of heating and cooling of air and its effects on weather and climate.

Extract One – What are we learning? The subject of science

John, the teacher, began the lesson by explaining to the children that they were going to discuss what they had seen in the museum to help them to 'try and go over some of the things you have done in science in the last two or three years'. His manner was pleasant and encouraging, and he offered detailed prompts to the children to remind them of the exhibits:

01   John   put your hand up if you, in the museum, pressed a button, held it down for thirty seconds and watched while the balloon was inside, who can describe to me ...

(general murmuring from children)

05   ... right, who can describe to me what happened, Phil, would you like to have a go ...

Child 1   sir , the air went into balloon, then the balloon went up, and it pushed it out, the air, then it went down ...

10   John   right, anyone else like to add anything to that

Child 2   hot air ...

(general murmuring from children; several begin to speak)

... when you held your finger down, you were pushing it out, and all the air went out of it

John   right, so you held it down for thirty seconds,
15   did anybody see what happened during those thirty seconds that you were holding it down ... ah

	Child 3	sir, all the hot air was going into the balloon
	John	hot air, how was the hot air going into the balloon
	Child 3	(*indecipherable*)
20	John	right, so when you pressed the button, these heaters came on, heated up the air, thirty seconds ... then what happened?
25	Child 4	sir, the balloon started getting filled with the hot air, and it went up, sir, then when the air started getting cold, it came back down ...
30	John	excellent, so when the balloon, when the air was hot, the heater had heated it up, the balloon went up, then when it cooled down you say the balloon went down, did it go down more slowly or quickly or about the same?
	Child 4	more quickly
	Child 5	no.
35	John	you thought quickly, slowly, right, well that's something we may not have time for ... right, that's one experiment, so the air was heated up, the balloon went up, and it came down when the air cooled down

In this first part of the lesson, the teacher is asking the children to describe what they saw at the museum. He asks a series of questions which all expect the children to recall in increasingly greater detail what they had seen several days ago. The conversation is linear and additive. The children who take turns in the conversation all add something to the cumulative account. This satisfies the initial requirement they were given (lines 04). There is no time to stop and think about differences in opinion or perception, as we hear in line 35. However, the child who earns the greatest praise is Child 4, who tries to move beyond description to an explanation of *why* events happened in the way they did. He talks about the balloon going up and down as the air in it warms up and cools down. At this stage of the lesson, it is unclear why this should be particularly praiseworthy. It is not until later that it becomes apparent that it is the teacher's aim to link the science work with what the class have been doing about rainfall in geography.

This is, indeed, the true purpose of this section, as John explained to me afterwards. But it is not made clear to the children at this point. John told me later that his main concern in this lesson was to cover topics that were likely to come up on the science SATs test. He was anxious to ensure that the children would be able to use any information they had access to in the test. In his mind, the topic of rainfall (done in the geography lesson) linked with the experiments seen at the museum (visited

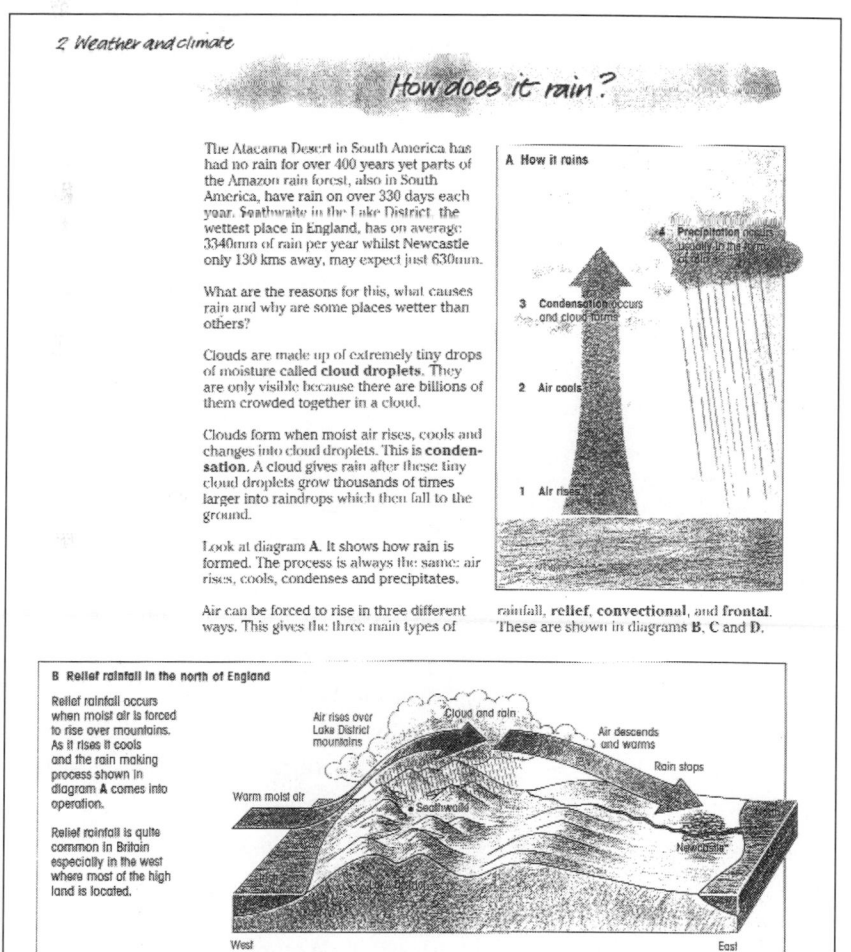

2 Weather and climate

How does it rain?

The Atacama Desert in South America has had no rain for over 400 years yet parts of the Amazon rain forest, also in South America, have rain on over 330 days each year. Seathwaite in the Lake District, the wettest place in England, has on average 3340mm of rain per year whilst Newcastle only 130 kms away, may expect just 630mm.

What are the reasons for this, what causes rain and why are some places wetter than others?

Clouds are made up of extremely tiny drops of moisture called **cloud droplets**. They are only visible because there are billions of them crowded together in a cloud.

Clouds form when moist air rises, cools and changes into cloud droplets. This is **condensation**. A cloud gives rain after these tiny cloud droplets grow thousands of times larger into raindrops which then fall to the ground.

Look at diagram A. It shows how rain is formed. The process is always the same: air rises, cools, condenses and precipitates.

Air can be forced to rise in three different ways. This gives the three main types of

rainfall, **relief**, **convectional**, and **frontal**. These are shown in diagrams B, C and D.

A How it rains

4 Precipitation occurs
3 Condensation occurs and cloud forms
2 Air cools
1 Air rises

B Relief rainfall in the north of England

Relief rainfall occurs when moist air is forced to rise over mountains. As it rises it cools and the rain making process shown in diagram A comes into operation.

Relief rainfall is quite common in Britain especially in the west where most of the high land is located.

Air rises over Lake District mountains
Cloud and rain
Air descends and warms
Rain stops
Warm moist air
Seathwaite
Newcastle

West
East

22

as part of the science lessons). There was indeed a clear conceptual link, but this does not seem to have been made explicit to the children yet.

Extract Two – How are we learning it? The power of the textbook

After the introduction, the lesson proceeded to a textbook-based phase lasting about 25 minutes. The children were asked to read (see page 93).

The following extract picks up the lesson at the point where the reading aloud from the textbook is about to begin:

	John:	sh-h-h-h ... now we're gonna have a look at this piece of writing here ... sh-h-h-h ... and we're gonna try and work out why I've talked about the experiment before we've done this, right,
05		number 1, when everyone's nice and quiet, could you start reading, please, (to class) once you've finished the title, make sure you follow .. Bilal
20	Bilal:	*(reads aloud first paragraph of page 22)*
	John:	right, could you look at the diagram at the
· 10		bottom of the page ... now, what we've just had read to us, and I hope you followed, Kylie, is the fact that some places in the
		world are very wet, and other places are very dry, for instance, in the desert, one desert, the
15		Atacama Desert, it hasn't rained for over four hundred years, right ... but in other places like the Amazon rain forest it's very, very wet, and ... em ... even in Britain, you get Seathwaite which is in the Lake District, that gets over
20		3,000 millimetres of rain each year, whereas Newcastle, right, that only gets .. 630 millimetres of rain each year, and the question today is why ... there is a reason, it's not just, well it's just like that, there is a reason, and it's to do with what we started off talking about,
25		it's to do with the fact, it's to do with the

balloon experiment, the experiment over there, right, and we're going to come on to that bit later on, alright, so, number two, could you read, please ...

30

The reading aloud is efficiently organised if somewhat regimented. But while Bilal is reading, many others do not follow in their books. Their eyes are wandering round the room or their heads are resting on their elbows. There is actually no real need for them to follow – after Bilal's reading, John repeats almost word for word the content of the paragraph

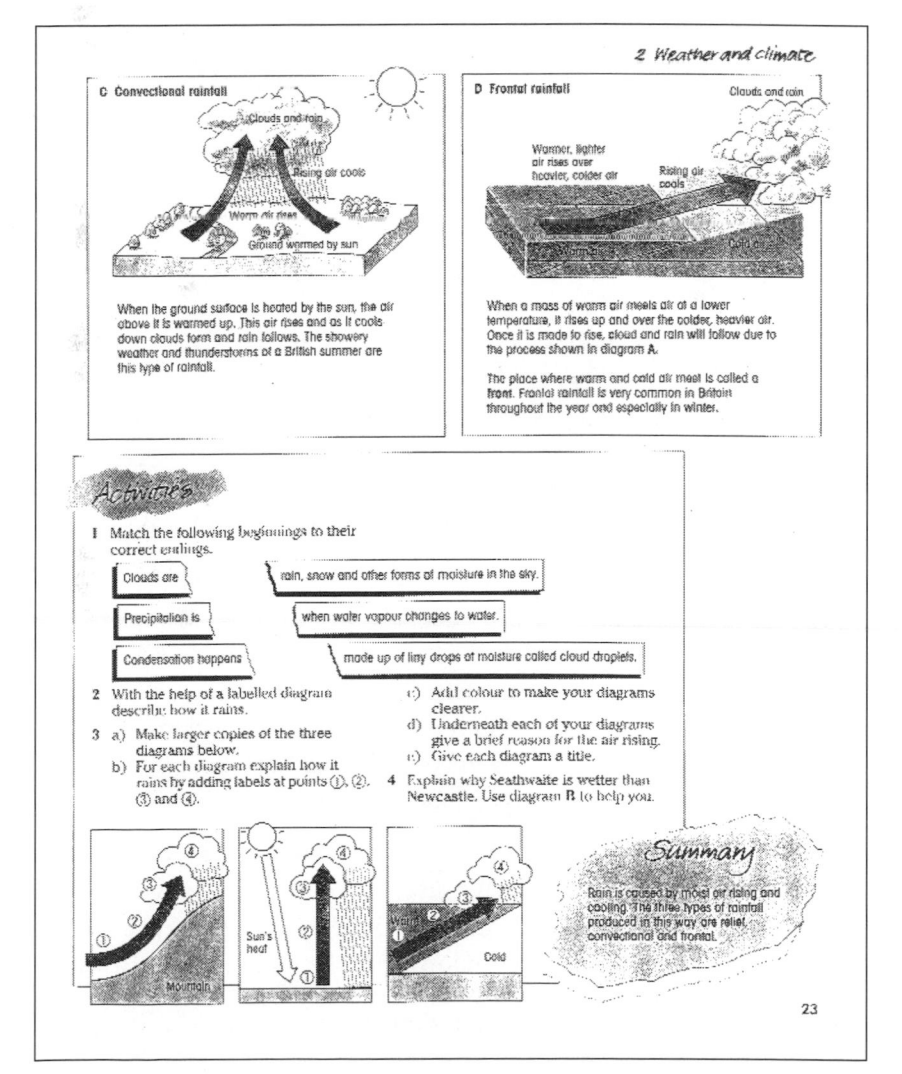

from the book. There is no discussion, though John does make explicit at this point the links with the visit and the content covered previously in science.

The reading aloud continues along the same pattern until all the paragraphs have been read. There is virtually no questioning of the children, no discussions about what the pages contain. The shape of the lesson is simple and linear. The whole thing is controlled and predictable. The science and the geography do link conceptually. The references the textbook makes to rainfall in different places around the world relate to the scientific 'fact' that warm air rises, demonstrated by the balloon experiment the children had observed in the museum. But the whole business of learning is surely much more complex than the structure of the lesson suggests. The textbook has, in effect, become the focus of the lesson. It provides the parameters for the legitimate knowledge it is transacting, each new chunk conveniently laid out over a double page spread. Apple (1993) comments on the 'power of the textbook' to contribute to the homogenising of the curriculum, to 'deprive teachers of a vital component of the curriculum process' and to lead to passive, transmission models of teaching and learning, and we can see that happening here.

Extract Three – Why are we learning it? The pressure for evidence

When the reading from the textbook is finished, the children spend about 30 minutes working individually to write the answers to the questions in the textbook. The relevant page in the textbook is reproduced on page 95.

While this is going on, there is a steady undercurrent of noise in the classroom, some of which is discussion about the questions. As they begin, John encourages the children to 'read the questions for yourselves' and to 'have a go and do the questions as best you can'. On page 97, you can see what Rehana produced in response to the questions.

We can see that she has reproduced several chunks from the textbook. She has done what she has been asked, looking for the answers within the two pages of the textbook. Her main guiding principle seems to have been to link words from the questions with the equivalent words in the text.

> How dose it rain.
>
> 1) Clouds are made up of extremely tiny drops of moisture called cloud droplets. They are only visible because there are billions of them crowded toghther in a cloud.
>
> 2) R Prep Precipitation ⌐ occurs usually in the form of rain.
>
> 3) Condensation appens
>
> 2) Precipitation is rain, snow and other forms of moisture in the sky.
>
> 3) Condensation happens when water vapour chan; in water.
>
> When the hot air raises, the air gets colder; After that it perfromes a cloud then the cloud gets heavear and rains; the cloud gets heav because the water gets colder.

When they have been working for about ten minutes, John calls the children to attention and says:

> ... now, most people have got the idea of this, one of the things I have been trying to get you to do for the last few weeks is read questions by yourself and try to work out what they mean so you can do the answer ... so when you're presented with an activity like this, the first port of call is for you to think, where's the answer most likely to be, so for number two it says, with the help of a labelled diagram, describe how it rains ... what diagram is most likely to help you to be able to do that, looking at the diagrams on the page?
>
> ...
>
> diagram A, which is called 'how it rains', so if you use your .. if you think a bit when you're trying to answer these questions, then you should be able to work out what they are asking you to do, then have

a think about whether you can do that or not, have a read of the text, the words, have a look at the diagrams, if you can work out what to do, then just do that, if you can't then that's when you ask for help...

The element of coaching is clear. John is preparing the children for answering questions in the test. He is making explicit to the children the ways he wants them to interrogate the text in order to answer the questions. He is also indicating strongly where 'knowledge' can be found. The answers to the questions (which have been validated as the legitimate knowledge for this lesson) are contained somewhere on the two pages. There is no need to go outside the confines of the book. This is what needs to be learnt. The children need to reproduce it in their exercise books as evidence that they have learnt it.

The lesson ends with oral feedback. John invites individual children to go to the whiteboard and report the answers they have written. Rehana is one of the children asked to do this. She begins by copying the answers she has written in her exercise book on the whiteboard. When John stops her, she simply repeats orally almost word-for-word what she has written in her exercise book. In return, she gets a housepoint. Rehana has successfully achieved what the teacher asked her to and has been rewarded. But this is a different kind of success from that she experienced in the first school. There is no evidence of the active learning or the collaborative talk she showed that she could enact so confidently in the Year Four classroom. Successful learning in the Year Six classroom has become a wholly different enterprise from what it was in Year Four.

This lesson was generally orderly and went at a good pace but John was not happy with it. Afterwards, he gave a negative evaluation of his teaching. He was somewhat hard on himself, as his rapport with the children was excellent, as was his presentation. He was aware of the tensions inherent in working within a system where it is necessary to produce measurable results and evidence while also being aware that children need to engage more actively in their learning in order to learn effectively. He explained that his intentions were to follow up the museum visit where the children had done some short scientific experiments, and 'to try to draw out some scientific information from these experiments they could use in a SAT test'. In a written comment later, he pointed out to me some of his frustrations with teaching science in Year Six:

... science teaching in Year Six in my opinion is more and more a tension between real scientific learning and cramming in the necessary facts to help them achieve L4 and this lesson probably didn't achieve either ...

John's frustrations are hardly surprising. He has absolutely no control over the curriculum he is expected to transact with the children. Those in control of the design of the curriculum have no first-hand awareness of the context within which John is working. What is needed is for teachers like John to be able to mediate the curriculum according to the context and the children with whom they are working. His views closely parallel the findings of the study by Galton *et al* (1999), which attempted to replicate the 1976 ORACLE studies into classroom interaction and the rôle of groupwork in children's learning. The 1999 study offered among its conclusions that:

... the introduction of the National Curriculum appears to have resulted in an increase in the traditional secondary style of teaching, creating a one-way communication system where, for most of the time, teachers talk and pupils sit and listen ...

I am not presuming to make value judgements on the quality of the teaching in either of the science lessons I have discussed at length in this chapter. I am less concerned with the pedagogy as a set of actions or skills to be judged than with the construction of the 'text' of the lesson in the nature of the talk and the opportunities this offers for the social construction of knowledge. In the first lesson, children and teachers collaboratively construct through their talk not only the knowledge to be transacted but also how and why it can be transacted. In the second lesson, though there is still the sense of a collaborative construction of a text, the form and content of this text is far more under the teacher's control. In the first lesson, there is evidence of the children appropriating through their talk the processes of knowledge construction, thus gaining power over their own learning. In the second lesson, this is not the case. Indeed, the teacher is not really in control of the knowledge either. It is externally mediated and then packaged within the textbook. By using the textbook, the means to knowing are kept under the immediate control of the teacher.

Many of the changes from the first lesson to the second have come about because of external pressures on the teacher to meet targets for the Key Stage Two SATs. While this pressure is more explicit in the middle school than in the first school, it is by no means absent in first school, as we will see in the discussion of the teachers' views in Chapter Five.

SUMMARY OF KEY ISSUES

In this chapter, I have provided a number of examples of talk in Key Stage Two classrooms between teachers, between teachers and children and among children. I have tried to show how the talk I have observed mediates the learning differently in different classrooms and with different teachers. Teachers and learners are always actively involved in these processes of mediation, but the lessons to be learnt vary. These are some of the key issues which have emerged in this chapter:

• The talk in the classroom is a major part of the social interaction, creating a culture of learning, not just a vehicle for the learning

• Collaborative talk, though difficult to organise in classrooms, is a highly effective means by which to develop children's conceptual understandings and their capacity to think

• The teachers' own views, personal experiences, knowledge and values are pivotal in constructing and understanding this social interaction

• Children's talk in classrooms is influenced by the ways in which talk is modelled and mediated by their teachers – listening to adult collaborative talk is a highly effective way for children to learn how to do it for themselves

• The clearly differential treatment of individual children on the part of the teachers needs to be recognised as a factor in individual children's success

• Externally initiated curriculum design and the pressures of external assessment can change the quality of the talk and the ways in which knowledge is negotiated in classrooms.

5

THE TEACHERS' VIEWS

So far, we have heard some of the personal experiences and views of the children and their parents about education and gathered something about the teachers' interactions with the children in the classroom. This chapter gives space to the teachers' voices as they express their opinions about the wider issues they believe can affect the learning of their pupils. It highlights some of the features within the second and third layers of interaction as shown in the diagram in Chapter One (page 23). It also illustrates some of the more general concerns teachers have about the system within which they are expected to work.

The relationships I developed with the first school teachers were different from those with the middle school teachers, mainly because of how the schools were organised. I got to know the first school teachers quite well through working in their class more or less every week for almost two years. We had many informal conversations about the children, the curriculum and the issues the teachers felt were significant to them in their work. Just after the children had transferred to Year Five in the middle school, I interviewed their teachers, Janet and Sandra, separately. Both gave generously of their time. The semi-structured interviews each lasted almost two hours and provide rich insights into the teachers' attitudes and their beliefs about their work and the children they taught. Though I visited the middle schools over two years while the children moved through Years Five and Six, I could not get to know the teachers there in the same way. This was through no fault of the teachers, who were open and friendly, but always very busy. There were also so many of them – the children were taught by twelve different teachers over the two years so their relationships with the children differed from those of the first school teachers, as the extracts that follow show. I got to know a few of the teachers informally through conversations in the staffroom and in between lessons. Then, when the children were about to transfer to Year Seven, I asked if any of the teachers who had taught them in Years Five and Six would be willing to be interviewed. This produced four enthusiastic volunteers, and we met after school one day for a conversation that went on for about two hours.

What all the teachers had in common was a great willingness to discuss and analyse their work, in the belief that this could improve what they were doing. They were all highly committed to helping the children to succeed. Also, to different levels and in different ways, they were frustrated and concerned by the difficulties they perceived as standing in the way of their helping the children achieve their full potential.

The first school teachers – social values and contradictions

Both Janet and Sandra almost always expressed positive attitudes towards the children and showed interest in their language and cultural backgrounds. They took an interest in the children's lives out of school and often invited them to share their home experiences in class. Janet lived near the school and had done so for a long time before she began teaching there. Sandra was not a native of Bradford had made a deliberate decision to seek a job there when she completed her training:

> ... I'm interested in the children, I mean I enjoy sort of finding out about them as well, you know they tell me things about their family and their background and their trips, I mean I'm interested in the children, you know the Asian children ... I mean that was my interest when I was at college ... that was actually my long study, you know ... my main subject at college was education in a multicultural society ... I wanted to teach in an inner school where there were lots of children from different cultures, I mean that's something that I really like ...

These positive attitudes affected their work in the classroom. Both teachers clearly enjoyed the time they spent with the children and valued the social aspects of learning. Sandra explained the reasons she liked to work at the school almost entirely in terms of the personal relationships she was able to build up with the children, and the way she valued and enjoyed them as individuals. Janet also expressed her sense of the importance of the social and affective aspects of the children's learning. At one point in my interview with her, I tried to encourage her to discuss the specifically linguistic and cognitive advantages of collaborative talk in the classroom, but she was not to be drawn. For her, the main benefits were definitely affective, summed up in her comment that it made the children 'feel important'. Both teachers clearly regarded the nurturing of the social and personal aspects of the children's experience as an important part of their rôles. Both continually stressed the importance of developing positive relationships with and among the children. When I asked them about the qualities they considered important for children to become successful learners, both listed personal and social factors such as an ability to cooperate, self-confidence and a willingness to listen, rather than more directly academically oriented qualities.

But these positive attitudes do not permeate all aspects of their work. When I encouraged Sandra to reflect on the National Curriculum and the National Literacy Strategy and their effects on her work, a strong feeling of discomfort crept into the discussion. Here is an extract from the interview at this point, which reveals some of the contradictions which Sandra seemed to feel towards these and other externally mediated demands:

01	Sandra:	... on the other hand, not that it's too restrictive, but I think sometimes that it's not necessarily appropriate for the children, especially that it's all levelled and you've children who are
05		supposed to be working towards level 3 or level 2, or one child should have achieved this and that at a certain age. And I find that it's quite difficult really because at times you feel you're teaching something because you have
10		to teach it at this stage and it's not necessarily

relevant to the children. Sometimes
the vocabulary, particularly for the children
with .. you know .. English as a second
language, it's so complicated that they're not
15   understanding it they're not getting the gist of
it, because most of it is words that they don't
understand. And you've got to have evidence
that you've done it and a lot of it .. we talk to
them about something and get them to write
20   about it and it goes in the file .. and you really
think, you know, I've done that for the sake of
doing it, for the sake of having some evidence
that I've done it .. and I know that the children
haven't really understood it, they're certainly
25   not going to be able to remember it in three
weeks because they haven't really understood
it now. But you've got to do it, and you can see
that there's something that would be much,
much better that they could be doing, you
30   know much more relevant to them at this
stage, I mean, some of the things that we had
to do .. and particularly, I think, you find this
in science , but in other areas as well, they're
just not ready for it ...

Tension is apparent throughout this extract. Sandra is conscious that the children may not understand the work they are being asked to do, but feels she has no choice – they just have to do it. She feels constrained by the way she interprets the requirements of the curriculum and she is painfully aware of its inappropriacy for the children she is teaching. But she uses the argument of language to justify this (lines 12-15), suggesting here that the problem is with the children's level of English rather than with the content of the work itself. She complains about the prescriptive way in which she thinks the curriculum should be taught and the way children 'should have achieved' certain targets at certain ages (lines 06-07). Then, there always needs to be 'evidence that you've done it' (line 22), leading to files of written work which don't seem to serve any other purpose. She sees no room for negotiation in what this curriculum contains and the way it has to be 'delivered'.

Sandra is articulating her personal understanding and experience of the curriculum. For her, it is narrow and constraining. She seems to regard it as undermining her professional autonomy, telling her what to do rather than providing guidelines within which she can use her professional judgement. She almost begins to express a lack of confidence in her own teaching ability, especially in relation to science (line 33). Yet as we saw in Chapter Four, she is a skilled and sensitive teacher. The problem is, arguably, that she does not own the curriculum in any sense. The official knowledge has been handed down to her in such a way that she believes she has no personal or professional control over it. This may not accurately describe the way the curriculum has actually been developed, but this is how she experiences it. Apple (1993) points out the negative effects of this model of knowledge for society as a whole, and particularly for children from ethnic minorities and argues that the curriculum should instead be open to negotiation:

> The curriculum then should not be presented as 'objective'. Rather, it must constantly 'subjectify' itself. That is, it must 'acknowledge its own roots' in the culture, history and other social interests out of which it arose.

In order to construct such a curriculum, the accepted definitions of knowledge need to be flexible so that they can be constantly re-examined and re-formulated. To help learners develop independence over their own learning, the curriculum needs to be mediated between teachers and learners in ways that recognise their different viewpoints and formative experiences. But more than this, it needs to be negotiated between policy makers and teachers themselves.

In the extract above, Sandra hints at difficulties she thinks the children face in their learning. Their main problem, she seems to feel, is their limited grasp of English. I was surprised when she said this, as she had always had a very positive attitude towards the children's language capabilities. Further on in the interview, she says much more about problems she feels the children face that affect their achievements in school. Here is an extract from this part of the conversation:

01   Sandra: increasing numbers of children who don't
                          seem to be able to listen .. listening skills seem
                          to be quite poor and there's probably a lack of
                          levels of maturity as well, which is something

05   to be said [about] those with the behavioural problems as well .. increased children with special needs .. um ..

         JC: and is that something you've noticed over the years?

10   Sandra: mm .. definitely, definitely, it's getting worse, definitely .. and I suppose to some extent, the level of the children who we've been getting into the class .. they're generally not functioning at the level that you would expect

15   of children of that age and that's a worry, especially when you're supposed to be preparing them for middle school, you think, well, middle school are going to have these children and they will expect them to do this

20   and this, and they can't do it because they've come in at this level and you can't possibly get them up to that level when they've come in at this level .. you can only do your best and move them on from where they are .. but, I

25   suppose that's a pressure to some extent, that the children are not working at the level that would be expected .. it's difficult, I think we have had a change in the .. not the catchment area but the housing within the catchment area

30   .. I think that might have some effect on it .. um .. children coming from different backgrounds .. um .. we seem to be getting more children who have been .. um .. you know, who have some sort of difficulties or .. um .. with

35   whatever .. um .. it's difficult for me to say really, at this point .. um .. I mean we've got .. I suppose we've got an increasing number of Asian children as well .. um ... with the language difficulties but it's not that, it's not

40   necessarily that I don't think .. um ...

JC:	By the language difficulties, you mean their comprehension of English ....
Sandra:	The children .. yeah .. but it's not that so much I don't think as as .. um .. more the sort of the
45	behavioural problems that they .. the learning difficulties other than the language difficulties

Sandra had told me that she looked for a job in Bradford when she left college because of her ambition to work in a 'multicultural' setting. But she confesses that as time passed she has found herself enjoying her work less and less. She finds it difficult to understand why this is so. In the extract above, she seems to be looking for the causes of this in the children themselves. Can it be that her problems somehow lie with them? She begins, in lines 01-07, to ponder on the question of the difficulties faced by the children. She points to four generalised failings in the children themselves: they can't listen, they lack maturity, they have behavioural difficulties and they have special needs – a somewhat daunting list, but none of it really specific. She sums up her anxiety in a general comment, in lines 13-14.

The choice of words here is interesting and quite unlike how Sandra chooses to talk about the children at other points in the conversation. She uses a kind of 'officialese' language which seems to depersonalise the children. They are 'not functioning' as expected and so, she continues, they are not meeting the expected *levels*. The word *level* seems to be highly significant. Sandra repeats it seven times in this short extract. The uses and meanings of the word *level* in educational discourse have changed greatly over the past ten years or so. Whereas it was hardly used in educational discourse before the days of the National Curriculum, it is now a much-used word in policy documents and the media as well as in teachers' conversations. It reflects the current concerns with standards and measurable evidence of progress. As we can see above, it is linked for Sandra with external pressure – the school had an OFSTED inspection during the time I was working there – and a sense that she herself is being judged. She has to provide quantifiable evidence of the children's attainment and pass it on to the teachers who will receive them in middle school. For her, this is almost like a public display of her teaching ability. It is as if, because of this necessity, Sandra is finding it difficult to see the children as individuals. In order for her to do her job properly, they all have to behave in the same way. She can no longer enjoy their distinctive personalities and the diversity of experience they bring to the classroom – one of her most important personal reasons for going into teaching in the first place.

In trying to account for the 'lowering' in levels of ability she has perceived in the children, Sandra goes further still. She struggles on, her own sense of the contradictory nature of her statements possibly reflected in the growing number of hesitations and unfinished sentences as she speaks. Logically speaking, some of her statements appear not to make sense; for example, she seems to imply in lines 29-30 that it is the housing in the catchment area that is changing, not the people who live in them. Her assertion in line 38 that it is the 'Asian children' who seem to be creating all the problems appears to be hard for her to say and she almost retracts it immediately afterwards. The children who give her great pleasure are now also the cause of her greatest professional concerns and anxieties.

It is too simplistic to suggest that Sandra is confused or muddled in her thinking, though the extract could be taken to indicate this. She is a skilled teacher with a sensitive, thoughtful nature and a deep commitment to the children. In these statements, she is revealing her anxiety about the abilities of the children to meet externally imposed levels of performance. As she says herself in the previous extract, she could think of much more appropriate things for the children to do. After all, she knows them and their interests and capabilities much better than the designers of the curriculum do. But, in her view, her ideas do not count. She is in an unenviable position, having been given the responsibility for providing evidence for something which it is probably impossible to demonstrate. What's more, she has no power to challenge it.

In addition, there is probably little in her training or professional experience which has prepared her for this predicament. She speaks enthusiastically earlier in the conversation about a section of her BEd course called *Education in a Multicultural Society*, and of making visits to 'multicultural' cities in England such as Bradford, Coventry and Leicester. But this has most likely equipped her with a model of multiculturalism grounded in a more general model of culture as fixed and static and of multicultural identity as to do with those who are somehow separate from mainstream culture. This model is inadequate to explain the complex contexts in which she is working. It is not the kind of model put forward by Nieto (1999) and advocated in Chapter One as helpful in understanding the ways in which an education system can construct failure for some of its participants. It takes no account of the economic and social pressures on some of the families of the children in Sandra's class, nor of the changing, unsettled nature of some of their life experiences. She is caught in a dilemma with no readily available way to explain her growing difficulties. Something is not working and she feels powerless to question the system itself, though it may be what is causing the breakdown. The only way Sandra can see to explain the situation to herself appears to be to find the children at fault. Somehow, it is they who must be 'getting worse'. In this, she is resorting to a *blaming the victim* response (Cummins, 1996). This is harmful to the children, but it is understandable. We cannot blame Sandra for it – she is herself a victim, in a different way, of the same system, which is counter-productive and very destructive for everyone involved.

Teachers are inadequately prepared for a challenging task. They have scant support in dealing with the complex issues they face on a day-to-day basis, many of which the central system does not even recognise. As she deals with the children in her class, Sandra is the one who has to find a way to 'make it all work'. This involves reconciling two conflicting sets of demands. First of all, she has to satisfy the complex language, social and cultural needs of the children. Secondly, she has to meet the targets imposed on her from outside the classroom and raise the children's attainments to the levels demanded. We can see from the extracts of their classroom conversations in Chapter Four how Sandra and Janet go a long way towards meeting the first set of demands. Through their teaching, they provide the means for many of the children in their class to succeed as learners. But in terms of targets such as school league tables, OFSTED, and other external evidence of 'success', they will continue to struggle, through no fault of their own. Trueba (1989) worked in contexts similar to those in which Sandra and Janet are working, and based his definition of success on the same theoretical bases as I am using here. He suggests that it is not the children or their teachers who are failing but that the problems lie in the wider system:

... If we assume, within this theoretical perspective, that all children normally succeed in learning ... it follows that failure in learning is 'systemic'. It is not an individual failure, but a failure of the social system to provide the child with the opportunity for social intercourse. It ... is a social phenomenon understandable only in terms of its own historical, economic and political contexts.

Just as some of the factors which enable children to succeed in school originate from outside the four walls of the classroom, so do some of those which prevent them from succeeding.

Making the transition – more contradictions
The children moved to middle school at the end of Year Four. Nahida, Parveen and Rehana all went on to the same school and were placed in the same class. With about 500 children on roll, it was much bigger than their first school. In organisation, it was closer to a secondary than a primary school. Like the first school, and unusual for Bradford schools, it was ethnically fairly diverse. The proportion of Pakistani heritage to other children was about 1:2. There were also small numbers of children of Indian and Bangladeshi heritage. There was a school uniform and Muslim girls were allowed to wear *shalwar kameez* in school colours. As soon as they arrived at the school, the children were set in ability groups for many of their subjects. Nahida, Parveen and Rehana were all placed in the top sets. They were taught by many different teachers as they moved through Years Five and Six.

While there was a positive and friendly atmosphere in the middle school, there was much more formality than in the first school. The children walked around the building in a more regimented way. They did not talk to their teachers much between lessons. Assemblies and other whole-school routines were more formal and there was less organised talk between children during lessons as part of groupwork. Most classroom talk was from the teacher to the whole class. Many of these changes came about because the children themselves were growing up, but there were other reasons too. Right from the beginning of Year Five, there was a feeling of pressure to achieve specific targets in the Key Stage Two tests in English, Maths and Science. The children were keenly aware of them from the start, and were constantly reminded of the need to follow instructions and to work hard in order to pass. I was struck by how every time I talked to the children about the work they were doing, they focused on the ways they were expected to do it rather than the content – the 'how' rather than the 'what'.

Many of the teachers had worked in the school for a long time and this showed in the way they talked to each other about the school and the children. There was a strong sense that they shared the same views and attitudes, and that they assumed others did, too. This was something I had noticed during my visits to the school, and it came out very clearly in the interviews. The teachers' talk displayed strongly collaborative features. It reflected their perceptions of belonging to a shared culture, as teachers in a 'challenging' school. As the interviews progressed, I became very much a listener to their conversation and rarely felt the need to intervene.

In the group interview, the teachers' conversation quickly moved away from concerns directly concerning the classroom or the school. It touched on a wide range of topics including 'forced' marriages, policing in Bradford and the position of women within the 'Asian community'. For the teachers, the 'Asian community' was evidently a homogeneous and undifferentiated group. They seemed to have little specific knowledge about the religious, cultural and language backgrounds of the children they taught. They perceived the worlds of home and school as totally separate for the children, and they worried that this must lead to conflict and confusion, as the following short extract illustrates:

01	May:	It makes you think, they must be very confused, these children, sometimes
	Hazel:	I don't think they're allowed to think, really
05	May:	but they see things here, and then they go home ...
	May:	everything's going to be a different way when they get home
	Hazel:	mmm ... mmm ..
10	June:	I think one of the biggest regrets is that they don't enjoy a full school life because of their commitments everywhere else, you know, I mean for example, at the end of term there'll be a party and a disco or whatever, and they're

15

not allowed to come to that because they've to go to the mosque .. we're going out on a visit, and they won't be doing that because they've to get back in time for the mosque .. every time you say there's a trip somewhere .. will we be back in time for mosque?

20   Hazel: because they go every night ...

The teachers' view of the influences of home on the children's education was rather negative. Home was 'another world completely', where 'they're very keen to preserve their own culture at all costs'. Islam was perceived as a dominant force in their lives. It created 'a big burden for these children' in that 'the mosque comes first and everything's controlled'. They felt that Islam was somehow used by the 'community' to exert powerful negative control over the children:

01   May: I would say that the hold on these children by the community and the families, if anything, is stronger than it was ..

        Hazel: it's fundamentalism, basically, I think it has a
05   hold in Bradford

        June: it's stronger than it was because of the fear of losing control, because these children as you say, third generation

The teachers singled out one of the girls, Nahida, for extensive comment. They seemed to regard her as different from the others, mainly – it appears – because she wore western clothes. This leads to a discussion about Nahida's circumstances and the reasons why she may be so different from the other Asian girls in school:

01   June: .. Nahida, I mean, I've never seen her in a
                        shalwar kameez .

        Hazel: well, Nahida wants to read the Sky News, this is her ambition .. oh well .. I thought, well,
05   good on you, Nahida

        June: and she never wears anything on her head, does Nahida, she's always in tracksuit .. what did she wear on non-uniform day?

	Hazel:	it's always western
10	June:	it's always western, whereas the others, you see, always wear *shalwar kameez* ..
	May:	her mum's very westernised ..
	Hazel:	I've never met Nahida's mum ..
12	May:	she might dress in their traditional outfits but she's a lovely woman, somehow you warm to her, I can't explain why.. she .. I don't think of
15		her as an Asian lady .. I don't mean .. that's not derogatory to Asians, but you know what I mean .. and her English isn't perfect, but it's
20		there .. and .. em ..
	Hazel:	you see, there are one or two like that, a handful, but the majority .. I think it's probably education ..

The teachers are making many assumptions. That Nahida wears tracksuits and does not cover her head is taken as evidence of her ability to avoid harmful Islamic influences. Similarly, that her mother wears 'traditional outfits' (line 14) is seen as in contradiction to the assertion that she is 'very westernised' (line 12). The teachers seem to perceive wearing Islamic dress to be a sign of the docility and passivity of the wearer – a common notion in much western media. In the same way, Bhatti (1999) discusses how the Asian girls in the secondary school she studied were stereotyped by their white peers as passive and obedient because they wore shalwar kameez in school. Conversely, if a Muslim woman or girl chooses not to wear it, this constitutes a daring act of defiance. But is this always true? Nahida and her mother read my analysis of the teachers' conversation and laughed. Nahida pointed out that wearing western clothes did not make her a different person. Her mother commented that I had eaten Asian food several times at her house but 'had not turned into an Asian' yet. She explained that the tracksuits were chosen to keep her daughter warm in school as she had suffered badly from colds when she was a small child.

Like the teachers reported by Shepherd (1987) in Chapter Two (pages 32-33), the group of four middle school teachers recorded here do not seem to invest any cultural capital in the out-of-school experiences of the children they teach. They seem to suggest that, in order to succeed in school, the children have to abandon, rather than build upon, their home cultures. In this, they differ from the first school teachers, Janet and Sandra. There is no evidence of the two-way communication advocated by writers like Heath (1982) and Gregory (1996) for maximising the positive effects of home experiences on school performance. Their attitudes to the children's home cultures and experiences make it harder for the children to succeed in school.

I do not want to blame the teachers in any way. Their intentions are of the best and their opinions sincerely held. They are dealing with complex issues in difficult circumstances but with precious little guidance. Like the rest of us, their views are influenced by typical national media coverage of Islam and the rôle of women which, at best, struggles to interpret complex issues for a mass audience, and at times draws facile but misleading conclusions. Such coverage is dangerous. It reinforces the perception that 'ethnic minorities', particularly Muslims, are different, divergent, outside of 'normal' society and so not like 'us'. It undermines attempts to place diversity where it should be, at the centre of discussions about educational policy and curriculum. As the teachers concluded their conversation about the three successful girls they had taught, they mused about the factors which they thought had helped the children to succeed. One closing comment was a powerful statement about their sense that successful learners needed to be like their teachers:

> I've only ever once, now I think of it .. heard .. we're in England now, so we'll do as the English do .. and that's from a girl's father at Hollyford .. and she was a super bright girl, you know .. very few like that .. and his attitude was ..no .. we're in England now, do what the English do ...

The teachers seem to be expressing the belief that being like the 'English' is a necessary factor for success in school. But the vital question for the teachers is who are the English? – what does being English mean to them? I am sure that if they were pushed to define what they meant, their view of Englishness would be quite different from the Asian father referred to above who expressed the opinion that his daughter had to 'do what the English do' in order to succeed in school. When I showed this extract to a colleague at college, a woman of Pakistani heritage, born and educated in England and a qualified teacher of several years' standing, she smiled and responded with another question, 'Am I not one of the 'English' too?'

These questions of ethnicity and identity go to the root of certain factors which militate against the success of many 'ethnic minority' pupils in our education system. What is surely needed is not somehow to mould all children to fit the static model of 'Englishness' that is perceived to be required for success in the education system, but to develop and broaden the model itself of what it means to be English. As teachers in a diverse and changing society, our understandings of identity and ethnicity need to be flexible enough to include the diversity of knowledge and experience which all members of our English society possess.

SUMMARY OF KEY ISSUES

In this chapter, I have presented the views of some teachers about the problems and issues they face in teaching children from an ethnic minority background. Though they are a very small group, their views are valid, and will be recognised by many other teachers working in similar circumstances. These are some of the key points which have emerged in this chapter:

• Many teachers do not share the cultural, religious and language knowledge and background of the children they teach, and they know little about these aspects of their pupils' experience

• Teachers feel pressured and constrained by external demands to ensure their pupils reach specific, and sometimes inappropriate, levels of attainment

• Teachers' judgements of their pupils' potential for attainment – particularly girls – can be strongly influenced by external characteristics, such as the clothes they wear

• There needs to be a widening of the model of what it means to be a 'successful' pupil in the English school system.

6

WAYS FORWARD – PRACTICES AND POLICIES FOR SUCCEEDING IN DIVERSITY

The last three chapters have given a profile of the learning and language experiences of a small group of successful bilingual and bicultural learners as they move through Key Stage Two in typical mainstream classrooms in Britain. We saw how their learning in school is actively influenced by their home and community cultures as well as by what happens within the four walls of their classrooms. We saw how the interactions in the classrooms between them, their teachers and their peers are crucially important to their success. Also important are their teachers' views about what constitutes successful learning and the constraints they feel in meeting the distinctive needs of the children because of the prescriptive nature of the system within which they are working.

This chapter and the next explore the implications of all this for both policy and practice. Within a framework which places diversity at the centre of thinking and planning in school, practical ways are suggested for teachers to help their pupils to succeed on a day-to-day basis in their classrooms. To help bilingual learners – indeed, all children – to succeed, we need to have two main aims in mind. First, we need to help them gain access to and control over the 'knowledge that counts'. As described in Chapter One, this is the knowledge made powerful by its inclusion in the curriculum. It is what children need to know in order to achieve high levels in the official tests and other forms of assessment which are so crucial for future success. Second – but just as important – we need to provide the support and opportunities through which children can develop into confident, independent, powerful learners by the time they leave primary classrooms, ready to continue their journey through the school system. In these two ways, we will be promoting success in diversity for all children.

As the principles of good teaching in any context should indicate, we need to use and build on the knowledge and skills that learners already possess in order to help them learn new things. In essence, this means finding ways of playing to the children's strengths. The ways in which bilingual and bicultural children succeed in learning are essentially the same as for any children. To a large extent, good practice for bilingual learners is good practice for all. But research has shown that there are also distinctive features of their experience and knowledge which need to be borne in mind when planning for their learning. This chapter discusses these features and suggests ways in which teachers in mainstream primary classrooms can weave provision for them into their practice. The last section considers how such provision can be developed and supported by appropriate policies at national and local levels. Just as we need to play to children's strengths in order to help them succeed, the policies which will best support teachers in this task are those which allow them the space and autonomy to develop their own strengths and confidence in their professional rôles.

This chapter, then, is about five issues:

- Using children's bilingualism as a strength
- Valuing and respecting home languages and cultures
- Encouraging the use of children's stronger languages in the classroom
- Encouraging family involvement in children's learning
- Developing policies for succeeding in diversity

Using children's bilingualism as a strength

The word 'bilingual' has many different definitions. There is not enough space to rehearse them all here. For a full discussion of the ways the word has been defined and the implications for education, see Baker

(1996). When I talk about bilingual children in this section, I have similar meanings to Pauline Gibbons (1991). Gibbons defines bilingual children as those who operate in more than one language domain but do not necessarily have full competence in any of their languages. This definition thus includes those children who are at the early stages of developing the skills and expertise that knowing a new language entails. It is important to remember that bilingual children are not all the same, that their knowledge, experience, strengths and needs are as varied and diverse as those of any other children. Some may be new to English when they begin school, others may already be conversant in it. Some may have limited knowledge of their first language. Some may not have any real experience of written forms in any language. Others may be orally adept and literate in several different languages.

In some sense and to some extent, we are all bilingual even though we may actually speak and write only one language. The vast majority of monolingual English speakers naturally and intuitively use different kinds of English as they move through the social contexts and events which make up their daily lives. For some, these varieties of English can be very strongly marked and may include different regional dialects, particular varieties for social settings and more standard forms for work. We all have access to a range of ways of using language and languages which depend on who we are speaking with, what we are talking about and the purposes of the conversation – in other words, we all have language repertoires. Bilinguals have the benefits of a greater range of choices in their repertoires than monolinguals. For all of us living in Britain today, the kind of English we need to succeed is the same. We all need standard English to show that we are well educated, to give us access to high-status employment, powerful positions and the opportunities to enjoy fully the privileges of living in contemporary British society. One of the main tasks of schooling is to provide the opportunity for all children to learn standard English, to add its high-status forms and functions to the language repertoires which they already possess when they begin school.

Bilingual children (that is, those who have access to more than one distinct language) have certain advantages over monolingual children in their learning. Baker (1996) and Cummins (1996, 2000) both provide full accounts of the research into bilingualism and its cognitive, affective and social effects. Both agree that being bilingual affords the

individual greater cognitive capacity and fuller knowledge and awareness about language than being monolingual. They see these qualities
as potentially positive learning assets for bilingual children. As well as
the cognitive benefits, there are cultural benefits. Many bilingual children gain enhanced self-confidence and social maturity from operating
in and between different cultures. These can be seen as strengths for
their learning. The examples I gave in Chapter Three (p. 43) of the children's informal talk show their 'pragmatic biculturalism' (Knight, 1994)
in moving between the diverse, and at times dissonant, worlds of home
and school. Knight advocates the fostering of the qualities entailed in
pragmatic biculturalism which, she argues, 'enable pupils to function
with greater skill and understanding within the mainstream culture
which controls their lives'.

But these positive qualities will only have a beneficial effect on children's learning in contexts which recognise and value their worth. Bilingual learners need classroom cultures which nurture their strengths
and allow them to develop additive – rather than subtractive – bilingualism. Their knowledge of English needs to grow from their knowledge of other languages, not replace it. It will grow best in classroom
cultures which offer the kinds of support they can recognise and respond to. Besides helping bilingual children to learn, such supportive
classroom cultures will help all children to learn and this vitally important point should not be forgotten.

The Schools Council Mother Tongue Project (1984) included seminars
with teachers involved in working with bilingual children. One of their
main conclusions was that supporting bilingualism had benefits for all
children in the school as well as the teachers and the school community
as a whole. They saw it as a central and strongly practical aspect of
developing a multicultural ethos in a school, involving strategies which
any teacher could use in their own classroom. This chart sums up their
conclusions and provides a useful summary of the benefits of supporting bilingualism (see opposite).

There follow some ideas, arranged in three general themes, for practical
ways in which teachers can help promote additive bilingualism and biculturalism in their pupils.

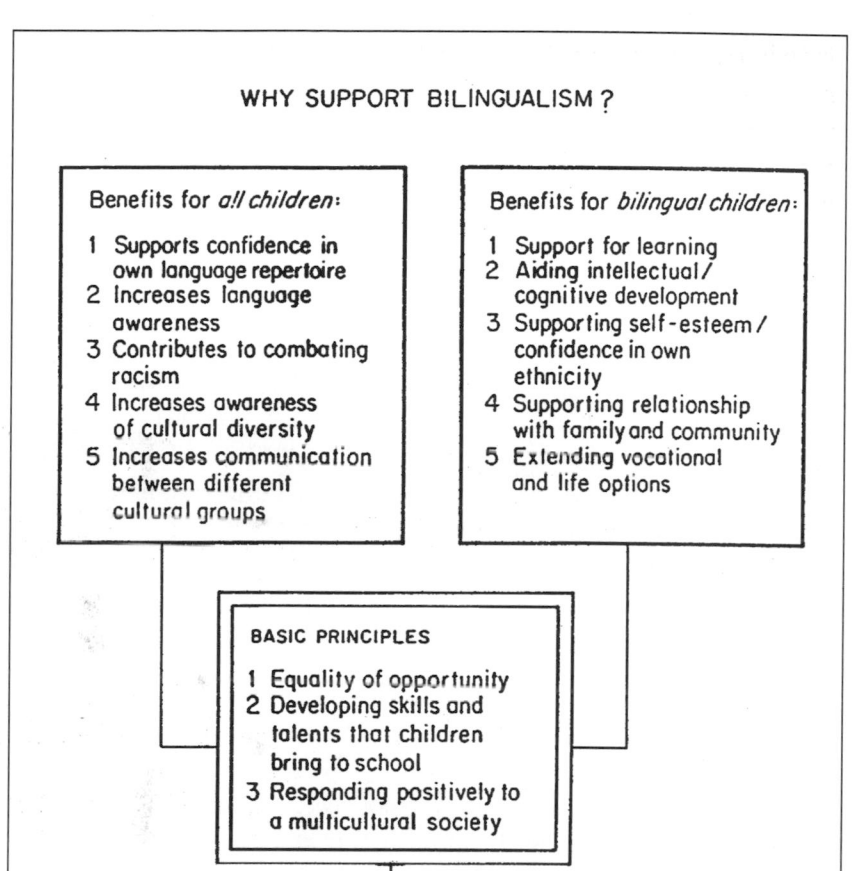

WHY SUPPORT BILINGUALISM ?

Benefits for *all children*:

1 Supports confidence in own language repertoire
2 Increases language awareness
3 Contributes to combating racism
4 Increases awareness of cultural diversity
5 Increases communication between different cultural groups

Benefits for *bilingual children*:

1 Support for learning
2 Aiding intellectual / cognitive development
3 Supporting self-esteem / confidence in own ethnicity
4 Supporting relationship with family and community
5 Extending vocational and life options

BASIC PRINCIPLES

1 Equality of opportunity
2 Developing skills and talents that children bring to school
3 Responding positively to a multicultural society

Benefits for *the teacher* and *the school*:

1 Increases knowledge of and relationship with individual pupils
2 Recognition of pupils' family / community as a resource
3 Increases teacher awareness of linguistic and cultural diversity
4 Strengthens school / community links
5 Contributes to multicultural ethos of the school

Valuing and respecting children's home languages and cultures

Rukhsana's story in Chapter One (page 22), with her powerful plea about the need to be herself as a learner, illustrates the dangers of ignoring the knowledge and experience children bring with them to school. In her case, she was able to overcome those early blows to her confidence which made her learning difficult as a young child. Some children are not so lucky. The knowledge and cultural experiences which they bring to school are ignored or regarded as negative and actively discouraged. No attempt is made to bridge the gap between home and school and it slowly grows wider. The effect of this is that children can move through school feeling either increasingly resentful and alienated or less and less confident about themselves and more withdrawn from what is going on around them. This happens not only with children who come from homes where the languages and cultural practices are different from school but also with those whose experiences of English at home lead them to know it as a very different language from that used and taught by their teachers.

A whole-school ethos which values diversity and respects the individuality of all the members of its community is vital for children's learning. To make sure these values are not marginalised and regarded as peripheral to the main concerns of teaching and learning, such an ethos needs to permeate the curriculum. The problem most primary teachers have with this is that they already feel the curriculum they are expected to teach the children is so full and prescriptive that it allows no space for individual variation. The result is that the 'valuing and respecting' gets squeezed into the corners. It tends to happen after the lessons have been delivered and the 'important' work has been done. A language-focused project carried out by a PGCE student on her final practice shows that this need not be so. It also illustrates how home languages and cultures can be valued and respected and given a central place in the curriculum in a simple and practical way.

Working with a reception class which included children from a range of language, cultural and religious backgrounds, Suzanne Aston decided to do some oral work. She noticed that some children were willing to speak out in front of the class while others were not. She also noticed that most of the talk was teacher-directed. The children did not find it easy to introduce and develop ideas of their own. The class was working towards the Early Learning Goals for Communication, Language and Literacy (QCA, 2000, pp. 45-67[1]). To help achieve these objectives, Suzanne decided to introduce the topic of names and carried out a 'Name Tree' project. This was a simple and imaginative idea which enhanced the children's learning a great deal.

Suzanne began by showing the children a photo of her own daughter and explaining how she had chosen her name. She then gave a letter asking for some information about the child's name to each child to take home to their parents. These were available in Urdu as well as English. All the parents responded positively. Some sent written notes into school and some spoke directly to Suzanne or the bilingual assistant. As the information came in, each child had a turn to talk about their name to the whole class. They were then helped to write the information onto a paper leaf for the name tree that had been put up ready on the wall. When appropriate, names were written in their original language and script. The children then hung their own leaf on the name tree. This took two weeks to complete. While it was going on, Suzanne introduced discussions about the names for different family members, illustrated her own family tree on the whiteboard and encouraged the children to talk about their families and to draw a family member.

By the end of the project, every child had stood up in front of their peers and teachers to speak confidently and at length, listened attentively to their classmates and taken part in discussions about family. The class also had an impressive name tree on display which parents were invited to see. Suzanne followed up the vocabulary development in more structured literacy hour-type activities, encouraging the children to read many of the words by sight. She sums up the positive outcomes of the project as follows:

> The learning gained from this valuable focused speaking and listening activity was firmly based in culture, religion, family and community. While children who spoke of their names did so with pride in front of their whole class, the children who listened did so with interest.

In her project, Suzanne shows how diversity can be placed in a central position in the curriculum, providing a strong focus for children's language learning, and potentially for other subject areas. The topic of names she developed with young children could be adapted for use with older children. They could analyse the spellings of their names, research their histories, compare names in different languages, consider different naming systems in different cultures and so on. Suzanne's work demonstrates how home languages and cultures can be brought into the centre of the curriculum and valued and respected as a natural and normal part of classroom life. Her work is underpinned by principles which enhance bilingual children's learning through focusing on their distinctive knowledge and which also demonstrate good pedagogic practice for all children. These principles can be summed up as follows:

- bilingual children need to feel that their languages and cultural and religious experiences are valued by their teachers

- different languages and cultural practices should be presented to all the children in the class as interesting and worthy of attention and study

- different languages and scripts should be evident in classroom displays, resources and signs as part of the ongoing, everyday work of the children

- the teacher needs to be willing to identify her (or him)self personally with the content and learning processes involved

- parents should be encouraged to participate in curriculum activities and share their own knowledge and experience with the class as a whole

These five statements together make up a useful framework for curriculum planning which places language diversity at its centre and shows that we value and respect the languages and cultural practices that children bring from home to school.

Encouraging the use of children's stronger languages in the classroom

There is strong evidence from research to show that allowing children to use their mother tongues in school has positive outcomes for their learning. This was a main finding of the MOTET project, carried out in Bradford and Keighley in the early 1980s (Fitzpatrick, 1987). Cummins (1996) also develops a powerful argument for the advantages of bilingual education. He bases this on his findings, which others have supported, that while it may take only two years for learners to develop full conversational and social fluency in a new language, it can take up to seven years for them to develop the capacity to use the language for cognitive and academic purposes. Skutnabb-Kangas (1981), through her poignant waterlilies metaphor, warns of the dangers of cutting children's cognitive development off at the roots by denying them access to their stronger languages in their learning. Gibbons (1991) suggests three significant reasons for allowing children to use their mother tongues in school. In brief, these are:

1. It allows children to draw on their total language experience, making it easier for them to develop understanding of basic concepts

2. It helps to provide a secure learning environment where children can develop confidence and self-esteem

3. It is based on sound pedagogic practice, taking advantage of one of the greatest resources children bring to school.

The term 'mother tongue teaching' is sometimes misunderstood. What I am discussing is more accurately described as 'mother tongue learning'. In advocating the use of children's mother tongues in mainstream classrooms, I am suggesting that we should allow children to use the languages in which they are most proficient as a tool for their learning. Their first languages can help them to learn the concepts and skills they need to know in different subjects across the curriculum and – ultimately – the English language. I am not suggesting that children should be actively taught those languages: there is no time for this in mainstream school, and it is not part of the school's responsibility.

The question of mother tongue use in mainstream classrooms is fraught. Most teachers who have bilingual children in their classes do not share their pupils' home languages. There are two large and legitimate concerns which such teachers often express on the matter:

•   how do I know that the children are on task, and not just chatting (or worse), when I cannot understand what they are saying?

•   how do I assess the children?

These are both valid questions. They indicate problems which cannot be ignored. The issues of power and control they raise are real concerns for any teacher. Children do use their home languages in classrooms to abuse each other and sometimes their teachers. They do so, I suggest, when they feel threatened and powerless, at odds with what is going on around them. But power and control are not always the same thing. It helps if we can see the differences between these two concepts. While it goes without saying that the teacher needs to maintain control over the discipline in her classroom, it is not always necessary or helpful that she retains all the power to decide how each child should be learning. I believe that if we deny children the opportunities to use the routes to thinking and learning which come easiest to them and are the strongest for them, we are denying them the access to power over their own learning. This is when children become uneasy and defensive, and their behaviour shows this. A classroom atmosphere which nurtures mutual trust and respect is empowering. It gives children the opportunity to develop power over their own learning and shows them how to use that power sensibly and with care.

The second question is perhaps easier to answer. Teachers are required to assess children's understanding and skill in English in various ways, as well as their conceptual development in a range of subjects. No one is expecting that we will assess children's knowledge of languages that we do not ourselves speak. In order for assessment to take place, the final outcome of an activity – for example, an oral or written report – needs to be in English. But the steps on the way to achieving that outcome do not all have to be in English. If children are allowed to talk and even write in their stronger languages as they are developing understanding of an idea or concept, their grasp of it will be stronger. One of the implications of this is that some bilingual children, especially in the early stages of schooling, may need more time to reach the desired outcome in English than their monolingual peers, but such time is always well-spent.

Even if we overcome concerns about discipline and assessment, allowing children to use mother tongues in the classroom is still a difficult area. It involves the understanding of complex ideas about language acquisition and learning. Study of these areas is not part of the required curriculum for trainee teachers and does not figure on most ITT or INSET courses. It is not surprising, then, that teachers are generally unaware of them. Also, teachers themselves often have limited personal experience of different languages and of language learning. Most of them do not share their pupils' experiences of bilingualism. And there are still far too few bilingual teachers who can identify with these aspects of their pupils' learning and perhaps inform their monolingual colleagues about ways of supporting and enhancing them. A useful introductory text in this area is Lightbown and Spada (1993), which explains with helpful examples many of the relevant theories of language learning and also discusses the implications for teaching and learning.

There are two stages to promoting the use of mother tongues in the classroom. The first is to create the kind of classroom culture described above, where mutual trust and respect are nurtured. Children feel empowered and both teachers and children feel it is safe to take risks. The second stage is to adopt a few practical strategies for allowing children to use their different languages in positive ways in their learning. Here, first of all, are a few suggestions to help teachers develop a classroom ethos where children can feel comfortable about using their stronger languages for learning:

- show interest in and find out about the children's home languages; the children themselves are often the best sources of information and will appreciate your curiosity

- invite children to teach the rest of the class how to greet each other in their languages, and use this knowledge as part of classroom routines

- make sure that your classroom visually reflects all the languages which its occupants speak in displays, resources and signs – some of these may be items which children bring in from home

- also make sure that these signs and resources do not fade and gather dust – change them regularly and, as far as possible, make them a feature of discussion and classroom learning

- make sure monolingual children regularly hear different languages spoken and see different languages written – use examples of languages they may hear and see in their local community

- allow bilingual children to listen to and (if they can) read stories in their home languages – they can make story tapes and books for each other and for children who do not share their languages

- use bilingual support staff sensitively and positively – demonstrate to the children that they are respected members of the class. As far possible, involve them in planning

- encourage bilingual support staff to take active rôles with all the children in the class, not just the ones perceived as needing extra support; for example, together you could read a dual-language story collaboratively for the whole class

Once a climate of trust and respect has been established, a few practical strategies can help children to use their languages positively to underpin their learning across the curriculum:

- for activities involving discussion, physically group children in ways that allow them to use their first languages with each other to help develop conceptual understanding

- give children time in these groups to talk to each other, then ask for a report or some other feedback in English

- build into as many activities as possible the opportunities for children to talk to each other about what they are doing in their stronger languages, eg allow pairs or small groups of same-language speakers to work together on practical or problem-solving tasks

- in whole-class discussions, invite confident speakers of different languages to contribute words and phrases as a check on understanding and reinforcement for children who may be struggling

- in Literacy Hour sessions, invite discussion about comparisons between languages on the ways meanings are expressed and words and sentences are constructed

As you gain experience and confidence in using strategies such as these, you will begin to think of ideas of your own which fit your own contexts. It is important, though, to sound a note of warning. The ideas listed above have been shown to work in that they can lead to significant improvements in children's attainment in SATs and other external assessments. But they are not always easy to introduce into classrooms where such strategies have not been used before. Suggesting to children that they can speak their home languages in the classroom can seem strange when the prevailing ethos has been that English is the only acceptable language. Children may feel self-conscious at first about using languages publicly which they normally reserve for more private and personal contexts. They may not understand why they are being asked to do so. This is why the first stage in the process – that of constructing a culture of value and respect – is crucially important. It can also be very helpful to share with the children the reasons why using their home languages can help their learning and make this knowledge explicit to them.

So far, I have focused on bilingualism in the modes of speaking and listening. I would like to end this section by mentioning literacy in different languages and scripts and their implications for children learning to speak, read and write in English. Many children in Britain – more than may be immediately apparent – are growing up biliterate, experiencing literacy in a range of languages and scripts as part of their everyday lives. Charmian Kenner (2000) documents the experiences of children in a multilingual nursery who confidently engage with different scripts in different ways for different purposes. In the late 1980s, the National Writing Project did valuable work in the area of biliteracy. In their publication, *A Rich Resource: Writing and Language Diversity* (National Writing Project, 1990), they provide examples of ways in which children make sense of all the different ways of writing they see around them. More than that, many children are becoming literate in two scripts at the same time as the following example shows (see page 130).

This is the work of Rujina, a six-year old child of Bangladeshi heritage who lives in London. It is a letter to her cousin in Bangladesh. Rujina is using all her funds of knowledge about writing here to write something important and meaningful to her. Those readers who can only read the English script can see that – like most six-year olds – she knows some things about writing but still has much to learn. Those who can read the Bengali script will see the same. In fact, Rujina is using the same strategies to try to make her writing meaningful in both scripts. In this, she is showing the ability to syncretise all the different ways of knowing about writing to which she has access. In the same way, the children in Chapter Three (page 46) are actively using the strategies they have gained from learning to read in English at school to help them make sense of a text they are reading in Urdu.

অইআা কর্ষ ডঅআা ইলব আা
কর্ইক বইক আব লঅব ক
বইঅব কইঅ কর্ষ ইনী

অই
অইক বইব
অইআা রিঢ়ে না- অই:

Dem My Ksu I DiD evn They
Ue ra gmu tos LDnD I
my soy hPoe Ther Ue ra
gMue   to   LDnD   awn   I
hPos   Ue   ra   RDe   a
Lta   to   Me
                       Love   FoMa   ✓   ✗
              RuJiha

There is much evidence to suggest that literacy in a first language helps the learner to develop literacy in a second. Think about your own experiences of learning to read English as a young child and then – perhaps – beginning to learn another language when you went to secondary school, which is a common experience in the British system. You will realise that your learning of the new language was strongly supported by your knowledge of the first. A bilingual teacher, completing her MEd, interviewed 'A' level students in a school in Bradford whose first language, both orally and in writing, was Urdu. Some of them had gained their early schooling in Pakistan and arrived in England when they were teenagers. It was clear that their learning of English depended heavily on the ways they had been taught Urdu. Gravelle (1996) gives examples of bilingual children whose literacy in their first language was clearly an advantage in their learning of English. In my own experience as a language support teacher with children in Years Five and Six, children who are literate in their mother tongue acquire skills and knowledge in English quickly and confidently, if the classroom context and circumstances allow it. The more teachers know about the experience of speaking, reading and writing the different languages children bring to the classroom, the more they can build positively on it to enhance their learning.

Encouraging family involvement in children's learning

Much has already been said and written about the need to involve parents in their children's learning. No one would now seriously question its value and the positive outcomes which normally ensue. At the same time, there has for long been a perception that it is difficult to involve parents from some ethnic minority communities, and even that some parents are not interested in their children's education. But the evidence from many studies shows that such a view needs to be questioned. Only a tiny proportion of parents are not interested in their children's education – and they are not restricted to any one social or cultural group. Bastiani (1997) reports examples of projects which illustrate positive 'home-school work' with ethnic minority parents and the benefits for children's learning.

The more significant issue is that some parents' own experiences of education have been very different from the mainstream British system. So, they may express their interest in different ways from parents who have themselves been through the system. This is something that Gibson (1987) found in his study of Punjabi Sikh families in California. Their children always gained high grades in school, but the parents did not attend school functions. Understandably – but mistakenly – their children's teachers took the parents' non-attendance to mean that they did not care about their children's education at all. This was not so: the parents were keenly interested and wanted their children to do well in school. They just did not realise the significance of the functions and it was never pointed out to them. The teachers, on the other hand, simply assumed that everyone would know.

There are two main dimensions to the area of home-school work:

- encouraging parents to come into school to discuss their children's progress and become involved in the work of the class

- developing ways in which parents and other family members can work at home with their children to reinforce the learning that is taking place in school

I do not intend to discuss the aspect of reporting to parents about their children's progress, as it is outside the scope of this section. It is also strongly defined by legal requirements and there is little room for schools to change the procedures they must have in place. Involving parents in the work of the class can have a much more direct effect on the quality of children's learning. Such involvement has generally tended to be about special events such as festivals, where parents have been invited to prepare interesting food to eat and perhaps bring in exciting artefacts for the children to look at. Such events are valuable and usually generate much positive interest. But they generally take place outside the normal routines of the class. Less easy to organise, but with more potential for enhancing children's learning, is the kind of work illustrated by Suzanne Aston's project about names. It is an excellent example of how parents' knowledge can be brought into the classroom and placed at the centre of the curriculum. In this way, it contributes to all children's learning, not just those who happen to be bilingual. It also demonstrates emphatically that the study of languages and cultures other than English is part of the everyday, ongoing work of a class.

Parents can contribute to many aspects of the curriculum in simple but important ways. Moll and her colleagues (1992) describe this as a 'funds of knowledge' approach. Schools actively find out about the kinds of knowledge which parents and families have and work out ways of taking advantage of it in the classroom. One area which has great potential is the parents' knowledge of their heritage countries. Rehana's story about Pakistan in Chapter Three (page 43) is an example of such a fund of knowledge. The class teachers made a feature of the experiences which Rehana talked about in one of their whole-class conversations. They also showed that they valued the information that came from her father about places in Pakistan, locating the places on a map and leaving it on display in the class for some time. Moll points out how teachers sometimes give high value to children's visits to countries in Europe and incorporate them into the curriculum. But the same regard is rarely given to children's family visits to their heritage countries.

Such work will only be effective if it is based on a firm foundation of positive communication between home and school. It is one indication of the strength of the home-school partnership which takes time and effort to develop and maintain. The fact that all the parents responded to Suzanne's initial request for information for the Name Tree project shows that she was working in a school where home-school links were well established. Faltis (1995) suggests that partnership begins with teachers stepping out of their classrooms to learn about the community in which they are working. This will give them the knowledge they need to consider how to involve parents in ways that are likely to harmonise with their other commitments and concerns. Raymonde Sneddon, in Bastiani (1997), suggests some of the simple ways in which schools can then go on to improve access for parents, including consulting about the timing of events, making sure that they are publicised in an appropriate way and so on. She points out how richly a little effort can be rewarded.

The second dimension of home-school involvement is about taking the school into the home. I called this section 'family involvement' because it does not just entail working with parents. Often, older siblings and members of extended family networks are better placed to understand what is happening for the younger child in school and to help mediate their learning experiences.

This happens in many ways. When I interviewed the parents of the children in the study, I came across many examples. The uncle of one of the children regularly sat down with his niece to discuss her school work and help her to make sense of it. One of the mothers I interviewed told me how she went through the times tables in Urdu with her four children. She was pleased to find that they could do them better in English. A father talked about how he explained to his children the way he had been taught to do long multiplication and division at school in Pakistan, which he thought was better than the way they were being taught in England. In most households the children regularly sat together in the evening to check each other's homework.

I have also learnt much about family involvement from students on our ITT and INSET courses. For her final dissertation, a bilingual fourth year BEd student chose to investigate children's experiences of oral storytelling in Punjabi and Urdu at home. She was inspired to do this by her own experiences of oral storytelling as a child and her questions about what they meant for her subsequent learning. She found out that many bilingual children in the Year One class in which she did her final practice spent a good deal of time at home listening to stories told by their grandmothers and retelling them among themselves. When they went to school, these stories were an excellent resource to help them make the transition from oracy to literacy in ways that writers such as Cramer, in Gregory (1997), describe. Another teacher, doing her research for her MA dissertation, asked some Year Seven children to keep literacy diaries. She asked them to record all the ways they learned and used different literacies at home and at school. The children documented endless discussions between older siblings – many of whom had left school – and younger ones. There was a great deal of transfer between languages and scripts.

These examples demonstrate how encouraging family involvement in children's learning gives mainstream teachers who work with bilingual and bicultural children many advantages. The children they teach have access to a vast range of learning opportunities. In their homes and communities, they are part of strong networks and cultures of learning. The whole family take part in the children's education, not just the parents. Often the older siblings are much more active than the parents in helping the younger ones. But their mainstream teachers seldom know about all this. They need to be helped to recognise that their pupils' school knowledge is only part of a wider whole, to see that there are more ways to help families support their children's learning in school than schools often generally tap into. Communication between home and school needs to be a dialogue, with exchanges going in both directions. The usual practices of sending reading books and other materials home need to be supplemented by information coming into school about what children are doing in different learning contexts.

Ways need to be worked about how this can be used to advantage. Again, diversity needs to come into the centre of mainstream schools' concerns, not be left at the margins.

There is another dimension to bilingual children's learning, mentioned in Chapter One (p.21). For many ethnic minority children in British society, formal learning does not end with the school day. Children regularly spend many hours in mosque, synagogue, church, temple, or community schools learning to read and write their heritage languages and the languages of their religions. I suggested in Chapter One that it would be excellent if teachers from the different schools could talk to each other, but I have never heard of this happening. If it did, perhaps they could contribute to building the bridges between children's school and community learning experiences. The holistic study of all these contexts for children's learning is a new and exciting field of educational research. Gregory (1997) and Gregory and Williams (2000) have researched the home, school and community literacy practices of Bangladeshi heritage children in East London. They interviewed a group of young Bangladeshi heritage women who remembered how they learnt classical Arabic and Bengali in community schools at the same time as learning to read English in mainstream classrooms. The ways in which they were expected to develop all these literacies at the same time were vastly different. One of the women summed them up as follows:

> Learning to read in English and Bengali was quite different. Bengali was more structured and you had to learn the alphabet and do strict spellings and do your homework, whereas in the English school you would learn through play and activities and have different topics and different areas.

Gregory and Williams also observed and talked to primary age Bangladeshi heritage children in their homes and schools. They watched the children playing school together at home, rehearsing the lessons they had learnt in school about maths, literacy and other subjects. The older children were helping and supporting the younger ones in engaging and impressive ways. Intriguingly, they were using strategies copied from both sets of teachers, Bengali and English. They were, in effect, syncretising home, community and school learning, using one to inform and enhance the other and in the process creating something new. Gregory and Williams argue that these bilingual and bi-cultural children gain strength in their learning from their access to 'contrasting literacies'. They have a 'treasure trove' of experiences on which to draw in their learning. The children are doing the job of building bridges between their experiences of teaching and learning that their teachers cannot do. In doing so, they are creating a new model of what it means to be literate, one that is richer, stronger and more dynamic than the old. It is a model that offers great potential for the future citizens of a world where hostility between different groups must be overcome and strength in diversity fully recognised.

Again, the implications for mainstream teachers are many. They could visit community places of learning and see for themselves the different worlds of learning that their pupils inhabit. They could invite their pupils to share with the rest of the class their different experiences of learning and what it means to them. Teachers' own awareness of the effects – both positive and negative – of their own use of language, particularly talk, on their children's learning are also important. Gregory and Williams briefly allude to this in their accounts of the classroom talk of the Bangladeshi heritage children's mainstream teachers. This too is a new area of research. There is growing evidence that teacher talk can provide appropriate cues and support for children, helping them to build bridges between their different worlds of learning. The conversations between Janet and Sandra described in Chapter Four are an example of this. The two teachers are together constructing a model for their pupils of ways in which talk can be used for learning. Similarly, Callender (1997) gives us a thorough and innovative analysis of the ways Black teachers use talk to tap into the deep-seated cultural knowledge of their Black pupils in beneficial ways for their engagement in school learning. These ideas are discussed more fully in the next chapter.

None of this places more demands on hard-pressed teachers. It may not be a case of changing what they do yet again, but of teachers recognising how their work in the classroom can harmonise with all the other things their pupils are busy doing. They can begin to evolve a new model of teaching and learning which genuinely places diversity at the centre. But teachers cannot be expected to do this in isolation and on their own initiative, along with all the other things which demand their time and attention. Relevant and supportive policies are required at both school and national levels.

Developing policies for succeeding in diversity

Gregory and Williams (2000) propose a model of reading success that harmonises strongly with the model of teaching and learning I have been developing throughout this book:

> It is a model based on the belief that contrasting rather than similar home and school strategies and practices provide children with a larger treasure trove from which to draw for school learning. The key task for teachers is to tap into this knowledge and to teach children to compare and contrast different languages and literacy practices. It is a model that is particularly relevant for children whose families do not share the literacy practices of the teachers and the school and whose reading skills, therefore, risk remaining invisible ... difference complements mainstream school literacy rather than opposes it.

Teachers themselves need personal experiences of difference in order to understand what it really means to be different. We need to try to position ourselves in the places where our learners are, to see things from their viewpoints. At the same time we need to try to see ourselves from the position of the learners, recognising the prejudices, shortcomings and limitations that we all have as a result of growing up in the society of which we are members. Despite the increasing diversity of British society, many of us have little direct personal experience of different cultures. We rarely have much to do with members of different groups in personal and private contexts on a daily basis. 'Multicultural' cities like Bradford have actually become more and more divided, with members of different communities living separate lives that hardly ever intersect, as discussed in Chapter Two.

As soon as we begin to appreciate the ways that different people make sense of the world and their place in it, two things seem to happen. The first is that we come to realise that their ways, though different, may be just as valid as our ways. The second is that we begin to recognise that we are all, in some sense, outsiders. We all have our differences, but at the same time we are all the same. Once we can see this, the differences stop getting in the way of our sense of belonging, both to each other and to a community, whether it be a school, a college, a street, a town or a country. Vivian Gussin Paley (1979) puts it like this:

> Those of us who have been outsiders understand the need to be seen exactly as we are and to be accepted and valued. Our safety lies in schools and societies in which faces with many shapes can feel an equal sense of belonging. Our children must grow up knowing and liking those who look and speak in different ways, or they will live as strangers in a hostile land.

In *White Teacher*, Gussin Paley documents her experiences in teaching classes of young children from diverse cultural backgrounds and her first experience of teaching African American children. Her personal 'difference' was that she was Jewish. When she began working as a teacher, this was not something she regarded as particularly significant. But as she learned from the children day by day about their different lives and experiences, she realised her own growing awareness of the importance to her of her Jewishness. This strong personal response helped her to see that it was impossible to treat the children as if they were all the same, that she had to recognise and respect the differences they represented. Just as she recognised her own need to be seen for who she was, she realised that their differences could not be ignored. Each child needed to feel they were welcomed and valued for who they were and what they brought to the classroom. The sense of belonging that it created was reinforced and enriched by everything that went on in Paley's classroom, among all its members, day by day. And what went on did not involve following some externally constructed scheme or complex strategies for teaching. It was, essentially, everyone getting to know each other and learning to get along through stories, music, art, walks and visits, language and number work. This is what a truly multicultural ethos should be.

Personal knowledge and experience of the issues is vital for all those trying to develop relevant policies that will support teachers teaching and children learning in diversity. Corson (1998) discusses such policy development at length. He points out how a 'one size fits all' approach can never work. Instead, he advocates an approach that recognises that inner city communities – like any others – have their own distinctive norms, values and cultural practices. These deserve the respect that any culture should be given. This stance helps us to consider issues of policy in an entirely new way. Policy makers must recognise that they cannot know all the answers. They must begin to pay attention to the 'multiple voices' reflecting the concerns of the teachers, parents and pupils who work every day in different ways in the communities. Corson suggests that for this to happen, decision-making is needed at all levels, from the centre to the periphery. It should happen at national, local and school levels rather than always at the centre, the way it does in England. In the same way as I have been advocating for teachers to allow the children in their classrooms the space to 'negotiate their own identities' (Cummins, 1996), teachers and others involved directly in working with children need the space to work out their own priorities in achieving the aims expected of them. We may all be expected to achieve the same goals, but we should have the right to work out our own routes to those goals.

Here is an example of a recently-qualified bilingual teacher working out her own priorities for her future professional rôle. Saiqa Riasat discovered something very important in the four years of her BA QTS course. She discovered that her education in mainstream schools had taken her far, but not entirely in the direction she wanted to go. She wanted to be rooted in her community, able to use her skills in a positive way to improve the lives of her community members. But first she wanted to test out all the lessons she had learnt during her course about supporting bilingualism, valuing children's home experiences and so on. So, for her final dissertation she decided to examine the arguments for and against using mother tongues to support bilingual children's learning. In her introduction to her dissertation, she eloquently articulates her reasons:

> It was only after embarking on my degree that I began to challenge my personal attitude towards my mother tongue and I started to make a conscious effort to break down the language barrier which years of schooling had created between me and my parents. Only when I realised that my mother tongue deserves the same respect as any other language did I begin to have respect for my culture and feel a sense of belonging within my language community.

The research she did convinced her that an additive bilingual approach was the most beneficial for children whose home languages differed from school. During her spare time she has set up a community-based class where she and a friend are teaching English to newly arrived children – some from the recent conflicts in Pakistan and Afghanistan – through their mother tongues.

Saiqa is certainly empowered by her knowledge. But will she have the opportunity to use it in the mainstream system to improve the quality of learning for her pupils in mainstream classes? Wrigley (2000) points out how schools are almost forced to employ a very top-down model of policy development and improvement, the one currently advocated by OFSTED. It requires strong leaders who work with speed and efficiency to hand down action plans and strategies to those beneath them. Wrigley argues that this is very much a 'control' model and is strongly reflected in the models of teaching and learning which underpin the recommended ways for teachers to work in their classrooms. But again, what is needed is not control but empowerment. Corson suggests that 'education for diversity' demands 'a use of power that is not only active and purposeful, but is also informed and emancipatory'.

He goes on to outline some of the ways in which 'emancipatory leaders' work. I summarise them here, as they embody principles which need to underpin policies to support education which places diversity at the centre:

- emancipatory leaders know when they are out of their depth: they recognise and accept the greater knowledge of colleagues in certain situations

- emancipatory leaders try to make their own presence a matter of small concern: they offer their opinions last rather than first

- emancipatory leaders remove the effects of their own power from the process of decision making: they accept democratic decisions and do not voice their own reservations or negative feelings

- emancipatory leaders leave the implementation of any decision to those to whom the task has been assigned

Perhaps the first step to developing policies for succeeding in diversity is the willingness by those in positions of leadership genuinely to try to practise these principles of emancipatory leadership. And as teachers, we need to be clear and confident about our own identities and beliefs and have our own vision of what we are hoping to achieve in the classroom, otherwise we are easy prey for the top-down policy-makers. We need to recognise our collective strength and power as we work collaboratively within schools and other institutions. Jim Cummins (2001) reminded us of this in his keynote lecture to the ninth NALDIC conference. He also went on to suggest a revisiting of the themes of the Bullock Report (HMSO, 1975) in relation to school policies. Despite the fact that it was written almost thirty years ago, Bullock still provides one of the best frameworks for language and learning in our schools and is worth careful reading and discussion.

Note

i   These are the Early Learning Goals in Communication, Language and Literacy achieved by Suzanne's project:

a)   Interact with others, negotiating plans and activities and taking turns in conversation

b)   Enjoy listening to and using spoken and written language, and readily turn to it in their play and learning

c)   Sustain attentive listening, responding to what they have heard by relevant comments, questions or actions

d)   Extend their vocabulary, exploring the meanings and sounds of new words

e)   Speak clearly and audibly with confidence and control and show awareness of the listener

7

STRATEGIES AND RESOURCES FOR
SUCCEEDING IN DIVERSITY

This book has shown the vital rôle played by language and culture in the processes of teaching and learning. Children's learning is rooted in and nurtured through language in many different ways. Learning in the primary classroom happens mainly in the interaction between children and their teachers and among children themselves. This is true for all children but aspects of bilingual children's knowledge and experience make their learning distinctive. A wealth of guidance and resources is available to teachers who are looking for ways of helping bilingual children to succeed in school. I have provided a short annotated list at the end of this chapter of some I have found particularly useful because they offer rich, practical ideas – firmly grounded in theory – for supporting bilingual children's learning.

But first I want to focus on two ways teachers can use language to help their bilingual pupils to succeed which are not really covered by other resources. The first is to do with approaches which promote talk as a resource for learning across the curriculum. The second is about using other aspects of language as resources to promote children's language development and learning – and also a genuine multicultural ethos – in primary classrooms, namely language diversity and literature. So this chapter has two main sections:

- talking and learning
- languages, literature and diversity

Talking and learning

As well to learning to talk in school, children need to develop the capacity to *talk to learn*. They need to learn how to use specific kinds of language in distinctive ways so as to construct for themselves through talk the knowledge they need to learn across the curriculum. They need opportunities for authentic discussion with their peers and teachers to help develop and reinforce their thinking and understanding of concepts in different subject areas. In her keynote lecture to the NALDIC conference (Gibbons, 2000), Pauline Gibbons argued that the two most widely accepted models of teaching and learning currently underpinning most policies and practices do not adequately recognise the importance of talk. Nor do they construct teaching and learning as socio-cultural processes – neither model places teachers and learners as part of a social group in a cultural context.

The view of teaching as *transmission* gives precedence to the rôle of the teacher. Learners are largely seen as passive recipients of the teacher's words. The *progressive* approach, on the other hand, places the child at the centre of the enterprise and the teacher at the edges as facilitator and manager. But both models view learning as occurring *within* individuals, not *between* them in interactions between teacher and learner. We need a new way to talk about teaching and learning that takes account of the central rôle of talk in all children's curriculum learning and especially in bilingual children's language development.

Gibbons has suggested a new approach, underpinned by three ideas about the nature of the processes involved and the relationships between teachers and learners:

- that learning is essentially a socially-situated, collaborative process
- that the rôles of teachers and learners are inter-related
- that both teachers and learners have active rôles in the whole process

These have strong parallels with Vygotsky's ideas about the essentially social nature of learning (see Chapter One, pages 4-5). They help us understand that teachers can use talk to scaffold not just the knowledge to be learnt but how this can be negotiated and co-constructed. The talk is – crucially – the evidence of the ways we need to think in order to learn as well as the medium within which the thinking is happening.

The talk can also help to extend the thinking and make it sharper and more analytic. Wells and Chang-Wells (1992) use the term 'literate thinking' to define this powerful outcome of effective classroom interaction. They argue that the development of such thinking is one of the main goals of education.

When I use the term 'collaborative talk' in this book to define the kind of classroom talk which offers children the best opportunities to learn in this way, I am drawing from Wells and Chang-Wells, who provide examples of what they mean by collaborative talk in multilingual classrooms. Mercer *et al* (1999) describe something similar when they discuss 'exploratory talk' and Corden (2000) uses the same term when suggesting strategies for promoting talk for learning in the Literacy Hour. The three-way classroom conversations initiated by Janet and Sandra (described in Chapter Four) are excellent examples of collaborative or exploratory talk between teachers and the whole class. The conversations with Parveen, Rehana and Nahida about science later in that chapter show a small group of children engaged in collaborative talk. Wells and Chang-Wells offer guidance for teachers on how to develop and participate in collaborative talk with children. Here is a summary of their main points:

- take what children say seriously and treat it as evidence of their best efforts to solve the problem in hand

- listen carefully to what children say and ask questions to help you correctly and fully understand the points they want to make

- in responding, take children's accounts as a starting point and extend and develop them or encourage children to do so themselves

- shape your contribution to what you know of each individual child's ability as well as your pedagogical intentions

- modify your contributions in the light of feedback provided by the children

Wells and Chang-Wells describe these guidelines as learning how to 'lead from behind'. They need to be made explicit to the children so they will also begin to adopt them in their interactions with others. After all, the whole process is meant to be collaborative. The guidelines could be shaped into some agreed ground rules to be used in whole-class, group or one-to-one situations. They could be displayed on a poster and referred to regularly as children become more familiar with these ways of talking and working. The process does not mean that teachers have to adopt a totally new way of working but rather a new approach to the way talk is managed and developed. An important first step in initiating this kind of talk – which, as Corden (2000) reminds us, is not always easy for children who are not used to it – is for teachers to share their intentions with their class.

Collaborative talk encourages the kind of active, analytic engagement that is so important to ensure that children fully comprehend the concepts they are learning. It can happen in whole-class, group or one-to-one settings. It is not how the class is organised that matters but the nature of the talk which ensues. Such talk fits in well with the pedagogical approaches advocated in the Literacy and Numeracy hours as part of whole-class input, groupwork or plenaries. Notice that in collaborative talk active *listening* is just as important as *speaking*. Both participants in the interaction are constantly actively engaged, whether or not they are actually speaking. This will not come naturally to many children and is something you will need to model, just as you might model a particular kind of writing. Once children have had the experience of hearing collaborative talk and engaging in it with adults, they can begin to practise it with their peers. Bilingual children will benefit immensely from using their stronger languages in small-group discussions, so organise groups to enable them to do this whenever possible.

As well as providing an approach which enables children to talk to learn, collaborative talk helps them to learn more about the language of the subject itself. It provides a framework in which the new technical and academic language connected with the subject can be introduced, revisited and refined. It fits well with the 'rich scripting' strategies described by Norah McWilliam (1998), where teachers are encouraged to consider as part of their planning the key vocabulary needed for a topic and ways of helping children to explore its possible meanings through the course of an activity. This is clearly important for bilingual children as it means they will meet new words more than once and can construct for themselves increasingly sophisticated understandings of their meanings and the ways they are used. Each subsequent encounter with a new word or idea helps guide learners along a continuum of language and conceptual complexity. Their knowledge of English improves through using the language in active and practical ways. They begin by talking about things in the 'here and now', embedded in the immediate context, and gradually move to talking and writing about them in the more accepted academic ways, where the language is usually disembedded from the context in which it is occurring.

This move from embedded to disembedded language and learning is in many ways like the move from oracy to literacy. In *Children's Minds* (1978) Margaret Donaldson argues that it is the key to formal education. Deryn Hall (1995) uses Donaldson's ideas to develop a framework for planning which ensures that children are constantly supported as they progress from contextually embedded activities to those which are disembedded from their surrounding contexts. Gibbons (1998) suggests a teaching programme to facilitate the progression from embedded to disembedded language. It has three main stages:

- *small group work*, where children engage in a task requiring authentic collaborative talk. There usually needs to be some kind of teacher input to the whole class to explain what is to be done and why before this can take place

- *teacher-guided reporting*, where each group explains to the rest of the class what they have been doing. The teacher introduces this with a focus on the kinds of language and the specific words the children need to use. While it is going on, the teacher encourages collaborative talk through questioning

- *journal writing*, where children work individually to record what they have learnt. This writing is the child's own personal response to the experience and is evidence for the teacher of the extent of their understanding of both the concepts and the language

This corresponds well with the 'three modes of interaction' which Wells and Chang-Wells regard, along with teacher exposition, as essential for effective learning through collaborative talk:

- sharing understanding (or ignorance)
- expert guidance
- reflection (through reading, writing or discussion)

It also links with literacy, for example having parallels with the process suggested to develop the KWL grids in the NLS training pack, Module Six, *Reading and Writing for Information*. The grids are essentially a frame to help children use information texts purposefully and analytically. They are centred round three questions, two to guide the specific goals of the research and the choice of relevant texts and the third for review and reinforcement:

- What do I already KNOW about this topic?
- What do I WANT to know about this topic?
- What have I LEARNT about this topic?

The kinds of language needed at each stage are different. They progress from informal conversation to more formal talk and finally to written language. The table below, adapted from Gibbons (2000), shows the progression with examples of language from a science activity about magnetism:

STAGE	LANGUAGE
1. Small group work (*children talking together in a group*)	try that ... won't work ... not metal these are best .. . go really fast
2. Teacher-guided reporting (*children reporting back to teacher and whole class what they have done in their group*)	we tried a pin .. a pencil sharpener .. some iron filings and a piece of plastic ... the magnet didn't attract the pin but it did attract the pencil sharpener and the iron filings
3. Journal writing (*children writing individually*)	Our experiment was to find out what a magnet attracted. We discovered that a magnet attracts some kinds of metal. It attracted the iron filings but not the pin.

As the children move through the stages, the support provided through the interaction allows them to try out new forms of language, with the focus always on trying to use it in meaningful ways for their own purposes.

In a classroom where there is genuine collaborative talk, there will be a recognition of the valuable contributions each participant is making to the interactions. Children are empowered, as are all the adults: class teachers, support teachers, classroom assistants alike. This has implications for the adults' rôles and for the relationships between them. In Chapter Four, we saw how when Janet and Sandra entered into collaborative talk with each other and the class, neither took precedence over the other and they modelled for the children how equal participants negotiate their meanings through talk. They had an effective partnership in their professional rôles which came about because of their mutual trust and the time they spent planning and evaluating their work together. Such partnerships take time and skill to develop but are essential to the ways of working suggested here. Jill Bourne and Joanna McPake (1991) defined partnership teaching as 'co-operative teaching plus' and described some of its elements as follows:

> ...the emphasis is on reviewing practice, setting short-term goals ... evaluating joint work ... It includes teachers working together outside as well as inside the classroom, to make the curriculum responsive to the language needs of all pupils.

Clearly, this has implications for the whole school. Teaching partners need time for planning and review. More than this, the approach to planning must allow teachers space to make their own professional judgements about the needs of the children they are teaching and to think about how to adapt the curriculum accordingly. Similarly, teaching partners need the freedom to make their own decisions about which approaches and strategies are best suited to achieve their objectives with the children for whose learning they are responsible. Partnership teaching needs to be a central aspect of a whole-school policy to support the learning of all the children. Bourne and McPake's materials offer guidance for schools keen to take on this way of working.

This section ends with a brief reference to the importance of story in developing children's literate thinking and confidence with language. Within the field of story I include personal narratives and storytelling as well as reading and listening to stories. Much has been said and written about this important aspect of language – Garvie (1990) and Gregory (1996) are two useful texts for teachers which give ideas for using story as a language and learning medium. Further details are given at the end of this chapter. Children's personal narratives and stories are important for the opportunities they give to the tellers to share something of themselves, their cultures and backgrounds in a safe and supportive context. As teachers, we also need to share these aspects of ourselves with the children we teach. In addition, storytelling is important for what it can show us of children's language and literacy development. Rehana's and Yasmin's stories (Chapter 3) demonstrate this. They are powerful evidence of their skill in constructing narratives and show that they can talk in a more sustained way and develop themes much more confidently than when they use other kinds of talk in the classroom. These are crucial aspects of children's literacy experience, as well as their oracy, and this must not be forgotten.

Storytelling is a different experience from story reading. It is more direct and personal. The teller is engaged in a creative act, making the story her own as she changes it slightly from the way it was told to her. It demands emotional engagement as well as control of story structure and language. Demands are also made of the listeners, who need first to agree to enter the world of the story and support the telling with attention and sympathy. Often, the participation goes beyond listening to include refrains, songs, body actions and so on. Good storytelling is richly satisfying but it takes practice. Children should have frequent experiences of telling stories and listening to the stories of others, children as well as teachers. Besides being entertaining, the direct, face-to-face interaction with no written text between speaker and listener helps to develop an atmosphere of trust and respect for other cultures and languages in the classroom. Shell's (1992) excellent compilation of ideas for working in multilingual classrooms, described at the end of this chapter, provides plenty of useful ideas for storytelling.

Finally, listening to well-written stories read out loud is an excellent language experience. It helps develop literate thinking, especially for children at the early stages of reading for themselves. It offers them exposure to good quality written language in a more sustained way than they would otherwise be able to read independently. As they listen, they begin to absorb its vocabulary, organisation and structure. They begin to internalise the patterns of literary language and recognise its distinctiveness from spoken language. They begin to appropriate these features of language into their own thinking and use them to enrich their own speaking and writing. Again, this is valuable for all children, but for bilingual children it can be even more beneficial. The next section lists some children's literature for reading aloud.

Languages, literature and diversity

Storytelling is also an important aspect of language diversity. Edie Garvie (1990) provides an excellent guide to using stories for language learning. The experience of hearing a story in a language which the listener may not fully understand is a valuable one. The sounds and rhythms of the new language are embedded in a familiar framework and enter the experience of the listener in interesting and memorable ways. Some skilled storytellers can make stories meaningful to their listeners even though they may not understand the words being used. Stories, then, are multilingual resources for all children. Dual language texts are the next best resource to bilingual storytellers, and also have certain advantages over oral stories in that specific features of the language can be more closely examined.

Dual language texts have been available for children in schools in Britain for a long time, but their potential as teaching resources for all children may never have been fully realised. A project carried out by the

---

'Rooikappie, Rooikappie!' roep Mamma.
'Ek het lekker koek gebak. Neem gou vir Ouma koek en vrugte.
Sy is in die bed. Sy is siek.'
'Ek kom, Mamma,' sê Rooikappie en sit haar pop neer.
Sy neem die mandjie en stap na Ouma se huisie in die bos.

Reading and Language Information Centre at Reading University (*Multilingual Resources for Children Project,* 1995) began to identify the value of dual language texts for both bilingual and monolingual children, not just for bilingual children alone. They can be excellent resources for language learning and also a resource to promote awareness of language diversity, multiculturalism and collaborative ways of working.

Dual language texts can work in these ways even if they use languages with which the reader is unfamiliar. On page 151 is a page from a dual language story book. You may know the language it is written in, though it is not commonly known. Can you read the text and identify the story?

If not, here is a picture which appears on the page beside the text to help you:

This is a version of *Little Red Riding Hood*. If you needed the picture to help you to work this out, go back to the text now and see how much more of it you can read, now that you know what the story is.

On page 154 is the same part of the story again, but in both languages as it appears in the book.

The language besides English on this page is Afrikaans. You may know that this was – and still is – the language spoken by the white Afrikaaners in South Africa and it became widely spoken throughout southern Africa. You may also know that it is based on Dutch, which was the native language of the Boers who originally settled in South Africa in the seventeenth century. There's a fascinating topic in history and politics here, but my main interest is in pointing out how much you can discover about Afrikaans and about language generally through this story book because of your knowledge of English and of the familiar story.

When I have done activities using the book with teacher education students – the vast majority of whom know nothing about Afrikaans when they start – they almost all manage to read the story in Afrikaans. This fact usually intrigues them and also helps them to see that meaningful reading depends on many things besides the words on the page. Some of them manage to translate the Afrikaans story into English. Some have also been able to work out some of the grammar of Afrikaans through comparing it with the English version. All this learning about language goes on while they discuss the historical, political, cultural and social issues around the development of a language like Afrikaans, which proves the point that you can't discuss a language without discussing its contexts.

I am not suggesting that Afrikaans is an appropriate language for work with children – it just happens to be the one in this particular story book. But there are ways you can use more widely available dual language books which use languages that may be spoken and written by students in your class. There are many such resources available and they need to be selected with care. *Building Bridges*, the publication of the Multilingual Resources for Children Project (1995), offers advice and suggestions for choosing and using dual language texts with all children. Here are some ideas for using three books which have been developed collaboratively by tutors and students at Bradford College, expertly sup-

'Red Riding Hood!' called Mother.

'I have baked some nice cakes.

Would you take some cake and fruit to Grandma quickly? She is ill and is in bed.'

'I'm coming, Mother,' said Red Riding Hood, and put down her doll.

She took the basket and set off for Grandma's house in the forest.

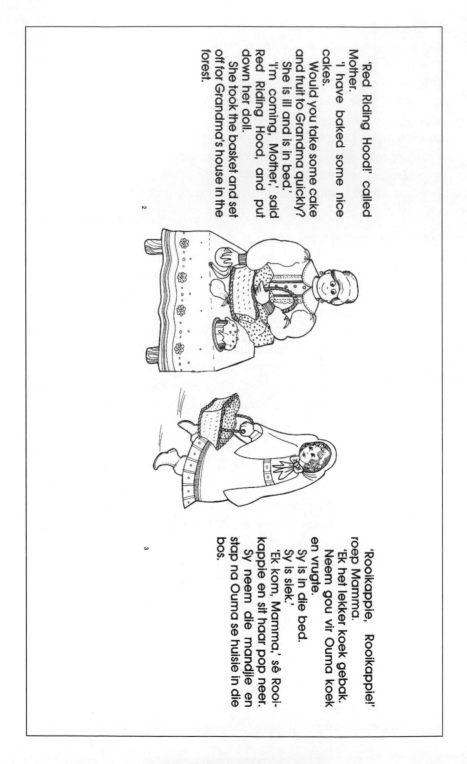

3

'Rooikappie, Rooikappie!' roep Mamma.

'Ek het lekker koek gebak. Neem gou vir Ouma koek en vrugte.

Sy is in die bed. Sy is siek.'

'Ek kom, Mamma,' sê Rooikappie en sit haar pop neer.

Sy neem die mandjie en stap na Ouma se huisie in die bos.

reached two hundred miles - to Peshawar in the north and in Lahore in the south. Naturally they attracted everybody for their happiness and prosperity.

Timmay.

That year, on the occasion of Eid festival, a great fair was held under the tree. All the girls from Lahore city flocked to get their colourful, ringing swings. They hung them in the mango trees and the girls in Peshawar did the same.

When their celebrations were at a climax, K2 began braying excitedly and closed his eyes. Now Mimi had some special Eid greeting on the houses at that time. Finally he could not tolerate the noise from K2. 'I'll fix that idle donkey,' he thought.

So out he came and lashed out at K2 with a rope. In his frenzy to save himself from the stinging pain, K2 turned sharply from east to west. And that is how the girls from Lahore came to be in Peshawar and the girls from Peshawar came to be in Lahore.

ported and advised by children, teachers, parents and others. They are in Urdu and English and all overcome the problems of presenting two scripts together which are written in different ways, as you will see. (All are available from the Department of Teacher Education at Bradford College, details at the end of the chapter.)

The Moving Mango Tree was written by Zohra Jabeen and illustrated by Georgia Woollard. It contains seven interesting, traditional stories from Pakistan. The English and Urdu versions are presented side by side, opening out from the 'front' and the 'back' of the book respectively, so that readers have a quadruple spread, often with a picture which relates to both texts, like this (see page 155).

The layout and size of the book mean it can be easily shared by a small group of children working together independently or as part of guided reading, or with an adult during a Literacy Hour session. It also allows the different ways in which the two scripts work to be discussed and compared. The stories could be read bilingually with two or more readers taking turns. Similarities and differences could be analysed between the traditional stories in the book and ones the children already know. Children could be encouraged to write similar stories of their own, using some of the elements of the stories from Pakistan.

Send for Sohail! came about through collaboration among some children in a first school, their teacher Maggie Power and students from college. The children's oral story was written down in Urdu and English and illustrated by a student. This time, the two languages are presented side by side on the page, sharing the illustration appearing on the adjoining page. The book opens from the top, which is unconventional for both scripts (see opposite).

This book also lends itself well to shared or guided reading in a small group. Having the two scripts side by side means they can be easily examined and compared – children can spot punctuation marks and other features they have in common and also look for patterns in the different scripts. You – or the children you are sharing the book with – may notice similarities between *Send for Sohail!* and a book in the Ahlbergs' *Happy Families* series, *Send for Mrs. Plug*. This is the book that gave the children the idea for their story and also a framework and some language to work from. This is an excellent way to develop stories with children and one which offers them a model as a starting point. Let

"Oh dear, oh dear!" they wailed,
"How can we get that elephant out of here?"
All the children playing outside in the
road knew what to do. They all shouted...

"Send for Sohail!"

Now whenever Sohail was sent for, he
always came, quick as a flash.

"An elephant - that's no problem," he
declared. And he took out of his pocket a
little mouse which he waved in front of
the elephant.
"Help!" trumpeted the elephant and he
squeezed himself out of the doorway and
charged back to the zoo.

ہائے ہائے اس ہاتھی کو ہم کس طرح ہہاں سے نکال
سکتے ہیں ؟ جو بچے سڑک پر کھیل رہے تھے ان سب کو پتہ تھا
کہ کیا کرنا چاہئے ۔ وہ دور دور سے چلّے ۔۔۔۔۔
سہیل کو بلاؤ!

سہیل جہاں کہیں بھی تھا وہ جلد از جلد آن موجود ہوا ۔ سہیل بولا
صرف ایک ہاتھی ؟ یہ کوئی بڑی بات نہیں ۔ اس پر اپنی جیب سے
ایک چھوٹی چوہی نکال کر اس نے ہاتھی کے سامنے ہلا دیا۔ اپنے آپ کو
دروازے سے نکال کر ہاتھی نے چنگھاڑتے ہوئے کہا مجھے بچاؤ!
اور سیدھا چڑیا گھر کی طرف بھاگ گیا۔

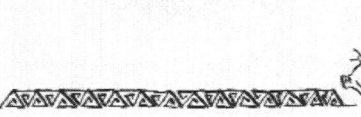

them choose an appropriate published story for themselves and develop their own version.

The last book in the set, *The Balloon Detectives*, was a joint effort by two students, Michael Jones and Michael Bailey. Michael Jones set out to write a story that also helped children to see some of the different ways we need to read to do things in everyday life. Readers have to look for clues in the text and illustrations, along with the two main characters in the story, to solve a puzzle. This time the English and Urdu versions are in two separate books held together by a paper band. They have the same illustrations and all the page layouts correspond, as you can see from this example from the Urdu version (on this page, and the correspondingly English version opposite).

As well as the Urdu script, the Urdu version has a transliteration where the sounds of the words are represented in the English alphabet. This means that children who can speak Urdu but not read the script can read

"کھلونوں کی دُکان کہاں ہے؟" "مجھے نہیں معلوم۔"

"Khilono ki dukaan kahañ hai?" "Mujhay nahiñ maaloom."

"ارے اس کے اوپر ایک خط ہے۔" "دیکھیں کیا لکھا ہے؟"

"Aray isskay upar ek khat hai." "Daykhaiñ kia likha hai?"

the story. Teachers or children who do not know Urdu can also 'read' it by saying the words as they are written. This may need a bit of practice but will lead to some interesting discussions about how things are said and written in different languages. It also affords excellent opportunities for children who can speak Urdu to teach others something about their language and how it works – thus promoting language awareness and also respect for others.

Literature can be both an excellent vehicle for language learning and a truly multicultural resource. Its power to move us beyond ourselves and connect us with the lives and experiences of others is well documented and recognised. But with the advent of the Literacy Hour, literature in primary schools has come to be viewed as predominantly a device for teaching aspects of *literacy*. Its true *literary* potential – its potential for developing affective, aesthetic and emotional responses in readers – is not always fully recognised and exploited. We need to be sure that we

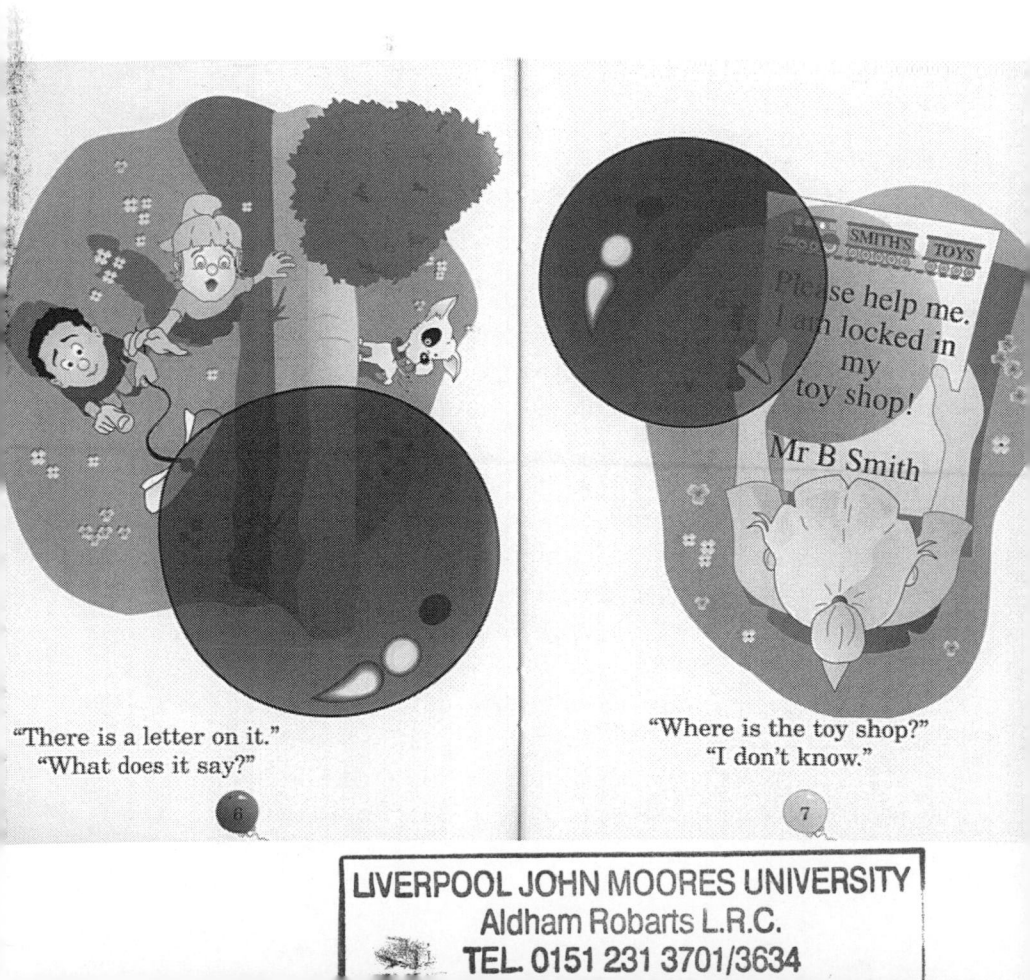

"There is a letter on it."
"What does it say?"

6

"Where is the toy shop?"
"I don't know."

7

fully understand what it means when we claim that literature is a multi-cultural resource. The Cox report (1989) made the first real attempt to define the purposes of literature in this way for the National Curriculum:

> ... literature in English should be drawn from different countries, so that pupils ... may be introduced to the ideas and feelings of cultures different from their own ... Not only should this lead to a broader awareness of a greater range of human 'thought and feeling', but – through looking at literature from different parts of the world and written from different points of view – pupils should also be in a position to gain a better understanding of the cultural heritage of English literature itself.

Other writers have added different dimensions to this model. Pat Pinsent (1997) talks about multicultural literature as those books which 'increase the flexibility of the mind'. Beverley Naidoo (1992) discusses the importance of readers 'being opened up to difference' through their encounters with texts which describe different cultures. The outcome for the reader is to change their attitudes and thinking so they develop:

- a greater capacity to empathise with the experiences of others
- an awareness of the need to challenge racist attitudes in others
- the development of critical thinking about the reader's own society and personal beliefs

The National Literacy Strategy suggests that teachers use 'literature from other cultures' as part of the range of texts they provide for their pupils. But 'literature from other cultures' and 'multicultural literature' are not always the same thing. And the way literature is mediated with children is important if we want it to achieve multicultural outcomes. Children can be introduced to stories, poems and other literature from different cultures in a way which merely emphasises their exotic nature and their distance from their own cultures. To make literature genuinely multicultural is to allow it to present and celebrate a different culture in an exciting way. More than this, it should offer an opportunity for its readers to recognise parallels with their own experience and to em-pathise with characters whose lives are very different from their own. It should help readers to recognise both their own individuality and their connectedness with the lives of others. This returns us to the quotation from Vivian Gussin Paley cited earlier (page 138). Through literature, we can encounter characters who may look and speak differently from ourselves but regard them as potential friends, not strangers.

There is a vast and growing range of children's literature available, as a visit to any bookshop or library will show. Try to get behind the displays of the biggest selling book of the moment to see the richness and diversity of what else is on offer. In choosing books for children, the first essential is to choose those which are powerful and meaningful for you as a reader. You need to be able to convey to the children something of the power the book holds for you. The best way to become familiar with the range and diversity of children's literature is to read as widely and greedily as possible. Local library sales can be an excellent way to get hold of children's books for a few pence – often those you can't buy in bookshops. I offer here a wholly personal and eclectic list of books which I would regard as resources for promoting a multicultural ethos. As you will see, many of them were written some time ago. Some may not be in print but will be available from libraries. The first set are mainly for Key Stage Two, but several would also be appropriate to read to Key Stage One children:

Books for reading aloud to children in Key Stage Two:

Bernard Ashley – A bit of give and take (1984)
Scott doesn't have much of his own and everyone seems to blame him when things keep going wrong. When he rescues a kitten from a rubbish skip, he is determined to keep it, despite the trouble it causes. Through trying to keep the kitten and to win a prize at school for helping old people, Scott finally proves his innocence of disturbing his elderly neighbours and makes an unexpected friend. Some Key Stage One children may also be able to read this book for themselves.

Betsy Byars – The Midnight Fox (1968)
Ten-year old Tom is very reluctant to go and stay on his aunt and uncle's farm while his parents go to Europe for two months. But when he gets to the farm, his encounter with the black fox with green eyes changes his attitude to the country, the animals and the people that live there for ever. When his parents come to pick him up after their trip, Tom is a much wiser boy. Many Key Stage Two children should be able to read this book for themselves.

Alice Dalgleish – *The Bears on Hemlock Mountain* (1952)

This is a simple story based on a 'tale told by the people' from Pennsylvania. Jonathan lives at the foot of Hemlock Mountain and is part of a large, extended family. When his mother asks him to go and fetch his Aunt Emma's giant stewpot from the other side of the mountain, Jonathan is a little apprehensive because of the bears. He keeps telling himself that there are no bears on Hemlock Mountain .... or are there? Some Key Stage One children may be able to read this book for themselves.

Anne Holm – *I am David* (1965)

Set at the end of the Second World War, this is the story of a boy who knows nothing but life in a prisoner-of-war camp on an island in the Mediterranean. His only protector, one of the guards, helps him to escape and he begins a long, solitary walk from the south of Italy to Denmark to find his mother. During his walk, he learns what it means to be human, and many of the people he meets learn much from him. This book may be challenging for some Key Stage Two children to read on their own, but many will love having it read to them.

Robert Leeson – *Smart Girls* (1993)

This is a collection of stories which all have girls as the main characters – smart girls all of them. The stories are based on little known traditional folk tales from different countries and are retold in a sharp, witty style that makes you smile, while the content of the stories gives food for thought. *Smart Girls Forever* is the follow-up.

Elizabeth Lutzeier – *Lost for Words* (1993)

Thirteen-year old Aysha has to leave her grandfather's house and all her extended family in Bangladesh to go with her father and mother to a new life in London. This life is not what she expects. It is hard, cold, disappointing. But through it all, she holds on to her grandfather's dream for her. This book will help children to understand what it is like to face life in a new country with 'no language', something which many newcomers to Britain have to do every day.

Beverley Naidoo – *The Other Side of Truth* (2000)

This is a powerful, superbly constructed novel which moves between Nigeria and London to tell the story of a brother and sister whose lives are cruelly disrupted by events in Lagos. Sade and her brother Femi are smuggled out of Nigeria for their own safety and their arrival in London sets in motion a frightening but plausible chain of events which reflect the complexity and danger of many children's lives in big cities today. Eventually, Sade and Femi are reunited with their father and together they are ready to face the challenges of the future. This book may be challenging for some Key Stage Two children to read on their own.

Philip Pullman – *The Firework-maker's Daughter* (1995)
Lila's mother died when she was a baby so her father, the firework-maker, makes a small cradle for her in the corner of his workshop and she watches the sparks fly and the gunpowder fizz and crackle while he works. As she grows up, the only thing she wants is to be a firework-maker like her father but, fearful of the danger involved, he refuses to tell her the final secret of firework-making. When Lila eventually decides to find out for herself, she sets out on a quest full of danger and excitement. But it is only when she returns to her father that she discovers the final secret and becomes a real firework-maker. Many Key Stage Two children should be able to read this book for themselves.

Louis Sachar – *Holes* (1998)
Stanley Yelnats has inherited the curse of his great-great grandfather which leads to his being accused of a crime he did not commit and sentenced to punishment at Camp Green Lake. Here, like all the other inmates, he has to dig a hole every day in the bare earth under the burning sun. The story weaves together incidents from the past and present and from different countries in an intriguing way. The reader quickly learns to spot the clues that connect the seemingly random events and the conclusion is immensely satisfying. This book may be challenging for some Key Stage Two children to read on their own.

E.B.White – *Charlotte's Web* (1963)
This story contains an unlikely combination of characters and events – a small girl called Fern, a pig called Wilbur, Charlotte the spider and a rat called Templeton are just a few. Fern's mission to remedy a 'terrible case of injustice' leads to a magical, rich, totally absorbing story of life, death and friendship which is warm, funny and sad. Through it, the animals which are the central characters show we humans how to live

and get along with each other. Many Key Stage Two children should be able to read this book for themselves.

And mainly for Key Stage One:

Maggie Glen – *Ruby* (1990)
Ruby is a teddy bear, but a very special one. As soon as she is made by the absent-minded Mrs. Harris, she has the letter 'S' stamped on her paw and is thrown into a box with other teddies, all of whom have 'S' on their paws. Ruby leads a mass escape from the box in the toy factory and during her adventures she learns that 'S' can stand for many things, but in the end it is what you make it that counts. This is a great story for children to listen to and read at Key Stage One. Children at Key Stage Two will also enjoy it and perhaps recognise more fully the levels of meaning it contains.

Bob Graham – *Crusher is Coming* (1987)
Peter has invited Crusher home for tea after football practice. He severely warns his mum not to kiss him when Crusher is there, and his little sister Claire to keep out of the big boy's way. But Crusher's responses to Peter's mum and little sister are absolutely not what Peter expects and make him – and the readers of this simple, clever story – realise that there are different ways of seeing things. This is another wonderful story for children to listen to and read for themselves at Key Stage One. Children at Key Stage Two will also enjoy it and perhaps appreciate its messages more fully.

Ann Grifalconi – *The Village of Round and Square Houses* (1986)
This is a story about a real village in an isolated part of Cameroon, West Africa. The villagers have found a way to live peacefully together, at times enjoying each other's company and at times having the space they need to be apart from each other. The little girl, Osa, hears from her grandmother the dramatic story of how the village came to be the way it is. The story is told in both words and pictures which need to be appreciated together for their richness and harmony. Both Key Stage One and Two children should readily access this excellent book.

Helen Piers – *Long Neck and Thunder Foot* (1982)

Long Neck's peaceful life is shattered when he realises he is not the only dinosaur in the swamp. Thunder Foot is around. Soon the two monsters reluctantly come face to face. Despite a show of strength on each side, neither can quite pluck up the courage to challenge the other. It takes a while before they learn that it is better to be friends than enemies, but finally they do and life is a whole lot better for all the animals in the forest. This is a great story for children to listen to and perhaps read for themselves at Key Stage One. Children at Key Stage Two will also enjoy it and appreciate more fully how its themes may relate to their own experiences of making and breaking friendships.

Reading is an interactive process. What readers themselves bring to the enterprise is crucial for their engagement with the text, their comprehension and response. If children are to develop into independent, enthusiastic and critical readers, they need the chance to choose for themselves texts which capture their attention and draw in their minds and their feelings. They also need opportunities to read for sustained periods of time. Such experiences are difficult to provide within the Literacy Hour format, so time needs to be found outside the hour for children to choose and share their own reading preferences. Children can also be introduced to reading journals so that they can record their experience of sustained reading during the Literacy Hour. This can work particularly well when children have grasped the basic skills of reading and need to consolidate these skills while developing independence and confidence.

Reading journals are notebooks in which children write down their responses and questions as they read a story for themselves at their own pace. Their purposes and use can be introduced to the whole class as part of a Literacy Hour session. The guided reading section of the hour lends itself well to sustained reading and the use of reading journals. Each reading group needs a book to read in class and children can be encouraged to take their copies home. Each day through the week, a different group works with the teacher, introducing a new book, discussing a current book or the content of the children's journals. The teacher focuses on the children's responses to their shared book and develops collaborative talk to encourage them to engage more fully with the themes and language of the story. The ideas suggested in *Teaching*

Literature 9-14 (Benton and Fox, 1985) are a useful guide. These are some of the questions that can be addressed – but there will be more:

• predicting from the first few pages what might happen further on in the story

• considering events from the viewpoints of different characters in the story

• speculating on why characters behave as they do

• thinking about the atmosphere of the story and how the writer uses language to create it

• expressing their own responses to the story's events, characters and settings

• noting down anything particularly exciting or interesting

• noting down anything they found confusing – to be returned to later as the reading progresses

When they are working independently during the Literacy Hour, the children can read quietly or write in their journals. In this way, the group can read several books together in a term and also choose books to read individually from a class box or the school library. The range of books offered may initially be fairly modest, but will grow with time and recommendations from independent child readers.

The power of literature to expand our horizons and allow us to hear the voices of others in compelling and illuminating ways needs to be reasserted in classrooms and made part of every child's education. In these times of increasing anxiety about 'otherness', when there is a danger of violent conflict because of our failures to engage and empathise with the concerns of others, we need every means at our disposal in the curriculum to allow children to experience and appreciate diversity. Events which arose during a session on poetry with BA QTS students illustrate this: it was part of a module on how to use poetry in the primary classroom. There were several bilingual students in the group, including some from China who were learning English through their study of primary education in our department. I organised the students into multilingual groups, then asked each group to share a poem or a story in a different language or perhaps a non-standard English dialect.

Collaborative talk soon filled the room. After a while, I asked each group to choose one text from the range they had been discussing and prepare to present it to the whole class. This proved interesting. One group gave us a rendition of the immortal ballad *On Ilkla' Moor Baht'at* in Yorkshire dialect – the Chinese members participating cheerfully. Another group asked if they could present two of their group's choices as they felt they complemented each other. The first to speak was a student who I knew was fluent in spoken and written Urdu. She stood up and recited Jinnah's *Prayer for Pakistan*, as he had recited it from the *Minah el Pakistan* in Lahore upon the country's independence in 1947. The rest of the class, most of whom could not understand Urdu, listened with rapt attention and applauded when she finished. Then another student stood up. I had not realised it, but she was Jewish, and she had recently begun learning Hebrew. She apologised for her lack of fluency in the language but said she would like to recite the *Prayer for Jerusalem*. She did so with growing confidence to a respectful silence from her audience. When she finished, the silence continued briefly, then one of the other students said, 'Don't the languages sound almost the same?' I agreed and we discussed how Hebrew and Urdu were indeed very similar. We talked about the similarities between the Muslim greeting *salaam alaikum* and the Jewish *shalom alechem*, both wishing peace upon the listener. After considering this for a while, another student asked, 'Then why are they fighting all the time?'

A third group had been grappling with issues of translation. Their Chinese member, Liu Juanhua, had introduced a poem in Chinese by He Zhizhang. Here is it:

回乡偶书
贺知章
少小离家老大回，
乡音无改鬓毛衰。
儿童相见不相识，
笑问客从何处来。

He read the poem in Chinese to the group and explained it in English. Then he offered them an English translation which he had found on the internet:

Coming Home
I left home young. I return old;
Speaking as then, but with hair grown thin;
And my children, meeting me, do not know me.
They smile and say, 'Stranger, where do you come from?'

The rest of the group decided to write their own translation of the poem. They asked Liu Juanhua detailed questions about the language in the original Chinese and looked closely at the Chinese characters to identify patterns and differences. This is what they came up with:

I left in my youth, I returned very old,
I still talk the same though my hair is white, not gold.
Children stand and stare, wondering who is there,
The question on their lips is 'Who? when? where?'

Not knowing any Chinese, I cannot say which translation is closer to the original. But it seems to me that, in the task they set themselves, the 'English' students were appropriating the meanings of the Chinese poem and giving them a shape and form with which they could identify more closely as poetry than they could the more formal English translation on the internet. Their version has rhyme, rhythm and an emotional appeal which might well correspond more closely to the feeling of the original. They certainly learned a great deal about poetry and about language from their task. Later, Liu Juanhua wrote modestly in his language journal:

> In my opinion, while translating Chinese poetry into English, it seems to lose some feeling and vigour. But if a Chinese who knows English very much explains it clearly, it would be much better.

I am not suggesting that translation should become part of the school curriculum, but I do believe that there is a place for poetry in different languages from which children can learn about language and culture and about others who may share their class, street, town or country. Again, it is a resource which – often – the learners themselves bring to the classroom and surprise their teacher. It allows us to appreciate the

STRATEGIES AND RESOURCES • 169

different ways in which we all respond to the same experiences of joy and pain and the ways we can share those experiences.

I end with a poem written a few years ago by a group of six-year old bilingual children who were all in the same class at Whetley First School in Bradford. We received it in college as an entry in a poetry competition we ran for schools. I would like to thank the children for producing such an excellent poem to illustrate the riches offered by placing language diversity at the centre and their teacher for allowing space in the classroom for the children to bring their knowledge to share. It is a poem about snow that begins in Urdu and is followed by the same ideas expressed in English.

Barf

Barf neechay artee hai
TIP TIP TIP
Barf bohot tandee hai
SSS SSS SSS
Barf syarda ho jattee hai
UPAR UPAR UPAR
Barf jam ja tee hai
CRIK CRIK CRIK
Barf saray jahan may hai
BOHOT BOHOT BOHOT
Barf gal jartee hai
TICK TICK TICK

Snow is falling
TIP TIP TIP
Snow is very cold
SSS SSS SSS
There is more and more snow
Layer upon layer upon layer
The snow has become ice
CRIK CRIK CRIK
We have snow everywhere
More and more and more
The snow is melting
TICK TICK TICK

Resources for teachers of bilingual children

This short list is of published resources which provide both practical and theoretical guidance – usually both together – for teachers seeking to promote multicultural, language-rich learning environments for children at primary level.

Garvie, E (1990) *Story as Vehicle: Teaching English to Young children* Clevedon: Multilingual Matters

Based on work with children and teachers in different parts of the world exploring how stories can be used as a resource for language teaching and learning, this book provides a thorough theoretical discussion about language acquisition and also many practical ideas about using stories as a learning resource.

Gibbons, P. (1991) *Learning to Learn in a Second Language* NSW, Australia: PETA

A concise and readable book which offers thoughtful, practical advice on supporting bilingual learners as they learn both English and other subjects in primary school. It is written for the Australian context where – similar to UK – there are many second and third generation bilingual children. Gibbons suggests specific activities as well as more general ways of organising the classroom and she helps the reader to recognise the generic principles of good pedagogy which underpin such activities.

Gregory, E (1996) *Making Sense of a New World: Learning to Read in a Second Language* London: Paul Chapman

Aimed primarily at Early Years teachers working in multilingual classrooms, the contents of this book will be valuable also for those teaching monolingual children and older children. Through fascinating detail about the learning experiences of children from a wide range of language and cultural backgrounds, the reader is introduced to an approach to teaching reading which encompasses what the child already knows – the 'inside-out'- and what is yet unknown – the 'outside-in'. There is a great deal of practical advice and guidance on resources for working with bilingual children.

Gussin Paley, V (1979) *White Teacher* Cambridge, Mass. and London: Harvard University Press

Not, strictly speaking, a resource book but an account of one teacher's experiences with a multilingual class in the United States of America. Paley records her day-by-day interactions with the children and shows how their learning is enhanced when they feel themselves respected and valued and they in turn learn to value each other. This short but powerful book shows how genuinely promoting multiculturalism in schools is very simple and at the same time vitally important.

Hall, D (1995) *Assessing the Needs of Bilingual Pupils: Living in Two Languages* London: David Fulton

A short, practical guide which addresses the issues about assessing bilingual children's language and learning needs. It deals confidently with the thorny problem of how teachers can differentiate the language and the learning factors and so avoid wrongly assigning bilingual children to SEN categories. It also provides a framework for planning based on the Cummins Cross which ensures that children always have appropriate support as they progress from embedded to disembedded learning.

Holderness, J and Lallje, B (eds) (1998) *An Introduction to Oracy: Frameworks for Talk* London: Cassell Education

Separate chapters by different authors provide practical advice and suggestions for supporting children's oracy in primary classrooms. The chapter *A Communication Framework for EAL Learners* has many useful suggestions for activities and is based on a model of additive bilingualism, though this is not explicitly discussed.

McWilliam, N (1998) *What's in a Word? Vocabulary Development in Multilingual Classrooms* Stoke on Trent: Trentham Books

Explores in depth the importance to children's learning in all curriculum areas of words and word meanings. It stresses the importance of vocabulary development as both a crucial aspect of language acquisition and the core to successful learning across the curriculum and provides practical advice on how to make both happen in multilingual classrooms. Photos and examples of environmental print remind us that words are a vital part of our worlds.

NALDIC (1998) *Provision in Literacy hours for pupils learning English as an additional language – a discussion document*
NALDIC (National Association for Language Development in the Curriculum) periodically produces short, informative papers on issues of current concern for teachers and teacher-trainers working with bilingual children. This title was compiled by NALDIC members who were involved in consultations about the implementation of the National Literacy Strategy. It provides a concise rationale and a discussion of the issues around working with bilingual children in the Literacy Hour and offers practical examples of EAL specialist teachers and class teachers working together.

Partnership Publishing materials
The three dual language books discussed in this chapter were produced by a group in the Department of Teacher Education at Bradford College. To find out more information and to purchase copies, contact the departmental office on 01274-751601

Multilingual Resources for Children Project (1995) *Building bridges: multilingual resources for children* Clevedon: Multilingual Matters, University of Reading: Reading and Language Information Centre
This is the report of the project based at Reading University which explored the range of dual language texts currently available and their use in mainstream and community schools. It provides useful guidance on the selection and use of dual language texts with both bilingual and monolingual children.

Shell, R (compiler) (1992) *Language works* London: Learning by design, Tower Hamlets Education
This short text is a collection of ideas for helping to teach bilingual children to read and write English using stories, games and other practical activities. It offers advice on shared and modelled reading and writing from the days before the National Literacy Strategy

Two sources for obtaining a wide range of multicultural resources:

Letterbox Library (www.letterboxlibrary.com), 71-73 Allen Road, London N16 8RY, tel: 020 7503 4801

A book club which specialises in children's books from all over the world with anti-racist and anti-sexist themes. A quarterly catalogue, which currently costs £1, is produced and a small membership fee means that you are entitled to discounts, special offers and so on

Multicultural Book Centre
(aamirdarr@multiculturalbookservice.fsnet.co.uk) Unit 33, Carlisle Business Centre, 60 Carlisle Road, Bradford BD8 8BD, tel: 01274 544158

Can supply every dual language text available in any language as well as books on a wide range of subjects for schools and other educational institutions. Aamir Darr runs a mail order service and also bookstalls at conferences and other events. He invites visits to the centre from school groups. He will advise on resources and source materials not in stock.

And finally ....
still the best way of keeping up date with children's books and having access to reviews and guidance in making selections is to subscribe to

Books for Keeps
6 Brightfield Road, Lee, London, SE12 8QF Tel: 020 8852 4953 (bboksforkeeps@btinternet.com)

BIBLIOGRAPHY

Apple, MW (1982) *Education and Power* Boston, Mass: Routledge and Kegan Paul

Apple, MW (1993) *Official Knowledge: Democratic Education in a Conservative Age* New York: Routledge

Arnold, H (1982) *Listening to Children Reading* London: Hodder and Stoughton

Baker, C (1996, 2nd edn) *Foundations of Bilingual Education and Bilingualism* Clevedon: Multilingual Matters

Bastiani, J (ed) (1997) *Home-school Work in Multicultural Settings* London: David Fulton

Benton, M and Fox, P (1985) *Teaching Literature 9-14* Cambridge: Cambridge University Press

Bhatti, G (1999) *Asian Children at Home and at School: an Ethnographic Study* London: Routledge

Bialystok, E (ed) (1991) *Language Processing in Bilingual Children* Cambridge: Cambridge University Press

Bourne, J and McPake, J (1991) *Partnership Teaching: Co-operative Teaching Strategies for English Language Support in Multilingual Classrooms – an Inservice Pack for Schools* London: NFER/DES

Bruner, JS (1996) *The Culture of Education* Cambridge, Mass: Harvard University Press

Callender, C (1997) *Education for Empowerment: the Practice and Philosophies of Black Teachers* Stoke on Trent: Trentham Books

City of Bradford Corporation (1970) *Education in Bradford since 1870* Bradford: Educational Services Committee, Bradford Corporation

Cole, M (1996) *Cultural Psychology: a Once and Future Discipline* Cambridge, Mass: The Belknap Press of Harvard University Press

Corden, R (2000) *Literacy and Learning Through Talk: Strategies for the Primary Classroom* Buckingham: Open University Press

Corson, D (1998) *Changing Education for Diversity* Buckingham: Open University Press

Cox, B (1989) *National Curriculum Working Group for English Report, English for ages 5-16* London: DES

Cummins, J (1996) *Negotiating Identities: Education for Empowerment in a Diverse Society* Ontario, CA: California Association for Bilingual Education

Cummins, J (2000) *Language, Power and Pedagogy: Bilingual Children in the Crossfire* Clevedon: Multilingual Matters

Cummins, J (2001) *What am I doing Here? The Rôle of Teacher and Pupil Identity in Developing English Academic Proficiency* Keynote address to the ninth NALDIC conference, Birmingham, November 17 van Dijk, TA (1993) Principles of Critical Discourse Analysis, *Discourse and Society*, 4(2) pp 249-283

van Dijk, TA (1999) Discourse and the Denial of Racism in: Jaworski, A and Coupland, N (eds) *The Discourse Reader* London and New York: Routledge

Donaldson, M (1978) *Children's Minds* London: Fontana

Driver, R; Asoko, H; Leach, J; Mortimer, E and Scott, P (1998) Constructing Scientific Knowledge in the Classroom in: Faulkner, D; Littlejohn, K and Woodhead, M (eds) *Learning Relationships in the Classroom* London: Routledge pp 258-275

Edwards, D and Mercer, N (1987) *Common Knowledge: the Development of Understanding in the Classroom* London: Routledge

Faltis, C (1995) Building Bridges Between Parents and School in: Garcia, O and Baker, C (eds) *Policy and Practice in Bilingual Education: Extending the Foundations* Clevedon: Multilingual Matters

Fitzpatrick, F (1987) *The Open Door: the Bradford Bilingual Project* Clevedon: Multilingual Matters

Foster-Carter, O (1987) The Honeyford Affair: Political and Policy implications in: Troyna, B (ed) *Racial Inequality in Education* London: Tavistock Press pp 44-58

Galton, M; Hargreaves, L; Comber, C; Wall, D and Pell, T (1999) Changes in Patterns of Teacher Interaction in Primary Classrooms: 1976-96 *British Educational Research Journal*, 25(1) pp 23-37

Garvie, E (1990) *Story as Vehicle: Teaching English to Young Children* Clevedon: Multilingual Matters

Gibbons, P (1991) *Learning to Learn in a Second Language* NSW, Australia: PETA

Gibbons, P (1998) Classroom Talk and the Learning of New Registers in a Second Language *Language and Education*, 12(2) pp 99-118

Gibbons, P (2000) Teaching as Mediation: Scaffolding Second Language learning through Classroom Interaction Keynote address to the eighth NALDIC conference, London, November 18

Gibson, MA (1987) The School Performance of Immigrant Minorities: a Minority View *Anthropology and Education Quarterly*, 18(4) pp 262-275

Gravelle, M (1996) *Supporting Bilingual Learners in Schools* Stoke on Trent: Trentham Books

Gregory, E (1996) *Making Sense of a New World: Learning to Read in a Second Language* London: Paul Chapman

Gregory, E (ed) (1997) *One Child, Many Worlds: Early Learning in Multicultural Communities* London: David Fulton

Gregory, E and Williams, A (2000) *City Literacies: Learning to Read across Generations and Cultures* London: Routledge

Gussin Paley, V (1979) *White Teacher* Cambridge, Mass. and London: Harvard University Press

Hall, D (1995) *Assessing the Needs of Bilingual Pupils: Living in Two Languages* London: David Fulton

Halstead, M (1988) *Education, Justice and Cultural Diversity: an Examination of the Honeyford Affair, 1984-85* London: Falmer

Harlen, W (1996, 2nd edn) *The Teaching of Science in Primary Schools* London: David Fulton

Heath, SB (1982) Questioning at Home and School: a Comparative Study in: Spindler, G (ed) *Doing the Ethnography of Schooling* New York: Holt, pp 103-13

Heath, SB (1983) *Ways with Words: Life and Work in Communities and Classrooms* Cambridge: Cambridge University Press

Hines, B (1968) *A Kestrel for a Knave* Harmondsworth: Penguin

HMSO (1975) *A Language for Life* (The Bullock Report) London: DES

Honeyford, R (1986) The Gilmore Syndrome *The Salisbury Review* 4(3) pp 11-14

Kenner, C (2000) *Home Pages: Literacy Links for Bilingual Children* Stoke on Trent: Trentham Books

Knight, A (1994) Pragmatic Biculturalism and the Primary School Teacher in: Blackledge, A (ed) *Teaching Bilingual Children* Stoke on Trent: Trentham Books pp101-111

Lightbown, PM and Spada, N (1993) *How Languages are Learned* Oxford: Oxford University Press

McWilliam, N (1998) *What's in a Word? Vocabulary Development in Multilingual Classrooms* Stoke on Trent: Trentham Books

Mercer, N (1995) *The Guided Construction of Knowledge* Clevedon: Multilingual Matters

Mercer, N; Wegerif, R and Dawes, L (1999) Children's Talk and the Development of Reasoning in the Classroom *British Educational Research Journal*, 25(1) pp 95-111

Moll, LC; Amanti, C, Neff, D and Gonzalez, N (1992) Funds of Knowledge for Teaching: Using a Qualitative Approach to Connect Homes and Classrooms *Theory into Practice,* 31(2) pp 132-141

Multilingual Resources for Children Project (1995) *Building Bridges: Multilingual Resources for Children* Clevedon: Multilingual Matters, University of Reading: Reading and Language Information Centre

Naidoo, B (1992) *Through Whose Eyes? Exploring Racism: Reader, Text and Context* Stoke on Trent: Trentham Books

National Writing Project (1990) *A Rich Resource: Writing and Language Diversity* Walton-on-Thames: Nelson

Nieto, S (1999) *The Light in their Eyes: Creating Multicultural Learning Communities* New York: Teachers' College Press

Norman, K (ed) (1992) *Thinking Voices: the Work of the National Oracy Project* London: Hodder and Stoughton

Pinsent, P (1997) *Children's Literature and the Politics of Equality* London: David Fulton

Pollard, A (1996) *The Social World of Children's Learning* London: Cassell

Rogoff, B (1990) *Apprenticeship in Thinking* New York: Oxford University Press

Ross, A (2000) *Curriculum: Construction and Critique* London: Falmer

Sharp, R and Green, A (1975) *Education and Social Control: a Study in Progressive Primary Education* London: Routledge and Kegan Paul

Shell, R (compiler) (1992) *Language Works* London: Learning by Design, Tower Hamlets Education

Shepherd, D (1987) The Accomplishment of Divergence *British Journal of Sociology of Education,* 8(3) pp 263-275

Shrubshall, P (1997) Narrative, Argument and Literacy: a Comparative Study of the Narrative Discourse Development of Monolingual and Bilingual 5-10 year old Learners *Journal of Multilingual and Multicultural Development,* 18(5) pp 402-42

Singh, R (1994) Introduction to: *Here to Stay: Bradford's South Asian Communities* City of Bradford Metropolitan Council: Art, Museums and Libraries

Skutnabb-Kangas, T (1981) *Bilingualism or Not: the Education of Minorities* Clevedon: Multilingual Matters

Street, BV (1993) Culture is a Verb: Anthropological Aspects of Language and Cultural Process in: Graddol, D; Thompson, L and Byram, M (eds) *Language and Culture* Clevedon: BAAL and Multilingual Matters

Tate, N (1996) Curriculum, Culture and Society Keynote paper at SCAA conference, London, February

Trueba, HT (1989) *Raising Silent Voices: Educating the Linguistic Minorities for the Twenty-first Century* Rowley, Mass: Newbury House

Vygotsky, LS (1978) *Mind in Society: the Development of Higher Psychological Processes* Cambridge, Mass: Harvard University Press

Vygotsky, LS (1986, new edn) *Thought and Language* (ed A Kozulin) Cambridge, Mass: Harvard University Press

Wells, G and Chang-Wells, GL (1992) *Constructing Knowledge Together: Classrooms as Centers of Inquiry and Literacy* Portsmouth, NH: Heinemann

Willes, MJ (1983) *Children into Pupils* London: Routledge and Kegan Paul

Woods, P (1996) *Researching the Art of Teaching: Ethnography for Educational Use* London: Routledge

Wrigley, T (2000) *The Power to Learn: Stories of Success in the Education of Asian and other Bilingual Pupils* Stoke on Trent: Trentham Books

Index